W9-CLC-868

PRAISE FOR *MASTERING BASIC CHEESEMAKING*

Gianaclis has taken the craft of cheesemaking and has molded it into another beautiful tome for cheese lovers. Her straightforward recipes will guide you through the exciting processes of crafting different cheeses, starting with the easiest then progressing to the more advanced recipes. She also shares some extra tips here and there to make the endeavor all the more successful. Whether you plan to make cheese or not! *Mastering Basic Cheesemaking* will help you understand how th ... mple ingredient — milk. Sh ... ke having her right there ...

... CCP™, author of ... heese including ... *Maître Fromager.*

"If only I'd ... ead *Mastering Basic Chee...* ... embarked on my own ch... ...nner's book is designed t... ...ion of recipes intended t... ...ng in the vat. This book ...

... CKEY, author of ... *getables & Herbs* ... *Relishes & Pastes.*

Over the ... much every book you ... ...ith *Mastering Basic Chee...* ...ng and creates another m... ...ess and makes it accessib... ...ugh many different styles ... ... realize how much you are learning until you get to the end and eat your creations. If you can use a cookbook, this book will show you how to make some great cheese... and also teach you how you did it.

— GORDON EDGAR, author of
Cheesemonger: A Life on the Wedge, Cheddar: A Journey to the Heart of America's Most Iconic Cheese and cheese buyer for
Rainbow Grocery Cooperative in San Francisco since 1994.

WITHDRAWN

10/16

Prairie du Chien Memorial Library
125 S. Wacouta Ave
Prairie du Chien WI 53821
www.pdcpuliclibrary.org

MASTERING BASIC CHEESEMAKING

MASTERING BASIC CHEESEMAKING

THE FUN AND FUNDAMENTALS OF MAKING CHEESE AT HOME

GIANACLIS CALDWELL

Prairie du Chien Memorial Library
125 Wacouta Ave.
Prairie du Chien WI 53821

new society
PUBLISHERS

Copyright © 2016 by Gianaclis Caldwell.
All rights reserved.

Cover design by Gianaclis Caldwell

All photographs © 2016 by Gianaclis Caldwell, unless otherwise noted.

Printed in Canada. First printing January 2016.

New Society Publishers acknowledges the financial support of the Government of Canada through the Canada Book Fund (CBF) for our publishing activities.

This book is intended to be educational and informative. The author and publisher disclaim all responsibility for any liability, loss or risk that may be associated with the application of any of the contents of this book.

Paperback ISBN: 978-0-86571-818-0
eISBN: 978-1-55092-617-0

Inquiries regarding requests to reprint all or part of *Mastering Basic Cheesemaking* should be addressed to New Society Publishers at the address below. To order directly from the publishers, please call toll-free (North America) 1-800-567-6772, or order online at www.newsociety.com

Any other inquiries can be directed by mail to:
New Society Publishers
P.O. Box 189, Gabriola Island, BC V0R 1X0, Canada
(250) 247-9737

New Society Publishers' mission is to publish books that contribute in fundamental ways to building an ecologically sustainable and just society, and to do so with the least possible impact on the environment, in a manner that models this vision. We are committed to doing this not just through education, but through action. The interior pages of our bound books are printed on Forest Stewardship Council®-registered acid-free paper that is **100% post-consumer recycled** (100% old growth forest-free), processed chlorine-free, and printed with vegetable-based, low-VOC inks, with covers produced using FSC®-registered stock. New Society also works to reduce its carbon footprint, and purchases carbon offsets based on an annual audit to ensure a carbon neutral footprint. For further information, or to browse our full list of books and purchase securely, visit our website at: www.newsociety.com

Library and Archives Canada Cataloguing in Publication

Caldwell, Gianaclis, 1961-, author
    Mastering basic cheesemaking : the fun and fundamentals of making cheese at home / Gianaclis Caldwell.

Includes bibliographical references and index.
Issued in print and electronic formats.
ISBN 978-0-9861907-0-4 (paperback).--ISBN 978-1-55092-617-0 (ebook)
    1. Cheesemaking. 2. Cheese products. I. Title.
SF271.C34 2015   641.3'73   C2015-906325-6
                                                  C2015-906326-4

CONTENTS

WHEN I BEGAN LEARNING how to make cheese late in 2002, there were just two cheesemaking books on the market — I bought both. I had been making yogurt, paneer, and butter since I was a young girl helping my mom in our farm kitchen, but cheese — real sliceable, meltable, grillable cheese — was a mystery to me. My desire to uncover the secrets of this tasty food came not simply from a passion for eating it (that was supplied in excess by my husband and youngest daughter), but from an ingrained mantra of "make and grow your own food — and do not waste." I knew that my family would have too much milk from our newly acquired, handful-size herd of goats, and I imagined that by turning the excess into a useful variety of products we could strike these items off the weekly grocery list and reduce the waste created by commercial packaging — a win-win.

The first batches I made, using Ricki Carroll's venerable *Home Cheese Making* (my favorite of those two initial tomes), made me feel as if I had performed magic — the alchemy of transforming humble milk into something entirely new and exciting. The sentiment was sustained and the pride of creation boosted by the passion with which my family and neighbors, who I had gathered for an impromptu cheese party, enjoyed the results. There is nothing quite as gratifying as pleasing others with food, especially a food steeped in tradition, mystery, and complexity.

Making cheese proved to be such a seductive and satisfying craft that in 2005 my husband and I began building our own *farmstead* cheese business, Pholia Farm Creamery (the name combines letters from the names of our daughters, Phoebe and Amelia). We relocated to a part of the old family farm where I was raised — twenty-four acres of woodland, mountains, and meadow — in my hometown of Rogue River, Oregon. Those were still the somewhat early days of farmstead cheesemaking, both as a skill and as a vocation. Friends and relatives were either reluctantly supportive or downright skeptical of our new venture. Even the local dairy inspector advised us that we would be better off to bury what little money we had in a tin can in the backyard. Fortunately for us, Americans' palate for fine *artisan* cheeses has continued to grow, along with the desire to eat locally and support small farms. My cheeses quickly achieved wide critical acclaim and we have always techincally been sold out.

In 2010 my first book *The Farmstead Creamery Advisor* (recently retitled *The Small-Scale Cheese Business*), was released by Chelsea Green Publishing. My second book *Mastering Artisan Cheesemaking* followed in 2012, and *The Small-Scale Dairy* appeared in the spring of 2014 (both also published by Chelsea Green).

Each of these books is meant to fill a gap in an industry of which I adore being a part. While it isn't easy to find time to write — now that our daughters have left home, our farm is run by just me, my husband, and when we are lucky, an intern or two — it is something that I find deeply fulfilling and well worth the effort of piecing together snippets of writing time. And I've happily found that milking goats and stirring milk in the cheese vat are useful times to ponder such things as chapter outlines and new book ideas.

Mastering Artisan Cheesemaking is a rather hefty volume, one meant to address the most complex of cheesemaking topics, and consequently not necessarily the best place for people to begin their cheese journey. Over the years, I have watched as the number of beginning cheesemaking books increased and waited for the perfect introductory guide. Unfortunately, the popularity of a topic does not always guarantee the quality of information available, and it has been with frustration and exasperation that I have reviewed most of these new publications.

While I love tackling advanced cheesemaking topics, when I teach beginning cheesemaking, I feel tremendous pleasure and joy. It reconnects me to my own first enchanting experiences with transforming milk into curd and curd into cheese. In this book I hope to share that magic, reveal its secrets, and guide you through the process in a way that no other book has done. You will be my private student, and I will be your personal trainer. Now let's get started and make some magic together!

HOW TO USE THIS BOOK

The first part of this book contains many details about the history, ingredients, and equipment of cheesemaking. You can read it first, last, or in between the lessons in the second part.

I structured the recipes, which I call "lessons," differently than in any other cheesemaking book. To get the most out of our lessons together, you should do them one at a time and in the order that they appear. If you decide to skip a lesson, you should at least read over it before moving on to the next one. Pay special attention to the Recap section following each recipe where we will compare what we just did with what we have learned so far. By working in this way, we will build knowledge and skills organically.

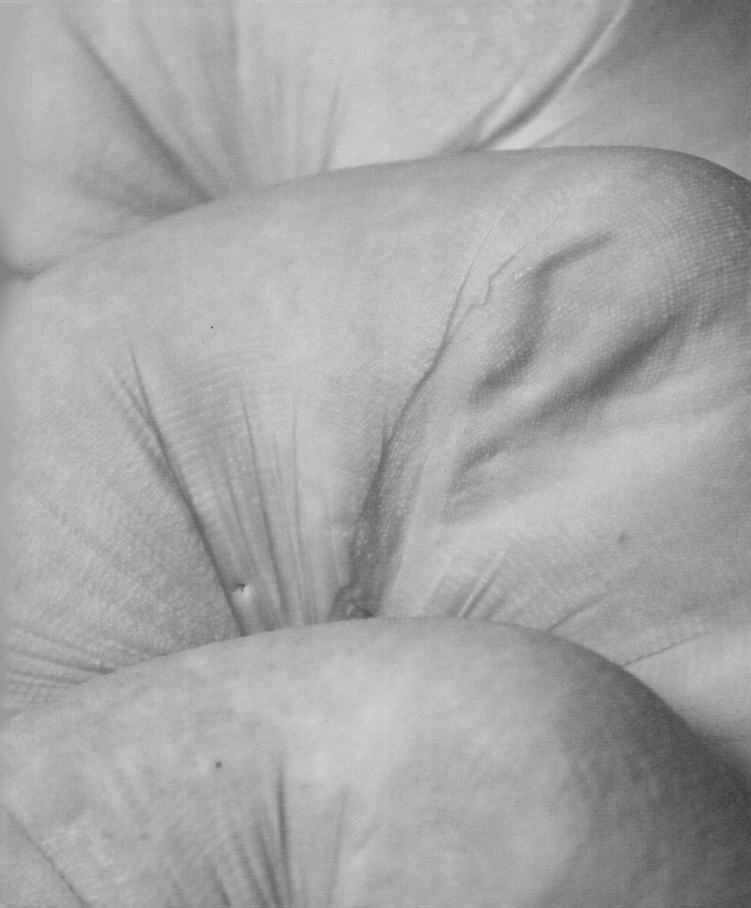

Part 1:

THE FUNDAMENTALS OF MAKING CHEESE

NOTES

1: WHY MAKE CHEESE?

AT ITS MOST FUNDAMENTAL LEVEL, cheese-making is meant to preserve milk. It is a way to feed our families during times of the year when fresh, nourishing milk might not be available. For some of us, it is also a way to make a living. But for many of us, cheese is not made out of necessity, nor because we can make it better than anything commercially available — and certainly not because it is easy. Primarily, we make cheese because we can. We make cheese because it gives us satisfaction. We make cheese because we love cheese.

Cheesemaking and milk fermentation can involve very few steps for simple, fresh cheeses or many steps for long-aged cheeses with complex flavor and delicious nuances. Either way, the process is fun, challenging, and fulfilling, and provides a link not only to long cultural traditions and foodways, but also to the earliest of our ancestors.

THE FIRST CHEESEMAKERS

Many of the best foods in the world involve some stage of *fermentation* — the process by which bacteria are allowed to act upon and change the food — including chocolate, coffee, cognac, and, of course, cheese. It is believed that fermented milk and beer were the first "processed" foods made by humans. (By processed, I mean that steps other than simple gathering

and cooking are involved, rather than what the term implies in today's convoluted food system.) Fermented grains, barley in particular, preceded fermented milk in terms of discovery and popularity (which is not surprising, really, since beer is still more popular than buttermilk!) Milk fermentation was likely discovered in the same happenstance fashion as beer: by being ignored. The milk of goats, sheep, and cows left to sit in prehistoric Tupperware (earthenware or tightly woven vessels) would have fairly quickly soured, thanks to bacteria naturally collected during milking, on the container and utensils, and in the air, changing the sweet, thin milk into a pleasant, tangy, slightly thick beverage.

This transformation of milk also provided a surprise benefit for our primitive ancestors, who had a problem when it came to milk: past early childhood they couldn't digest milk sugar (*lactose*) because they lacked *lactase*, the *enzyme* necessary to break it down. Many modern humans, too, lack this enzyme. For some, though, the enzyme that our stomachs produce when we are infants continues to be produced into adulthood and beyond. For those that do not make this handy enzyme, fermented dairy products, especially aged cheeses, are much more digestible because the bacteria in them breaks down the milk sugar before they are consumed.

The fermentation or souring process also makes milk much more tart than when it comes out of the animal. Where there is tang (not the orange-flavored powdered beverage famously promoted by astronauts in the 1960s), there is acid, and where there is acid, there is preservation. Foods that are high in acid don't spoil as quickly as those that are low in acid. This also made fermented milk of high value to our forebears.

It is believed that the next evolutionary step in cheesemaking, the use of a *coagulant* to thicken the milk beyond what simple souring could do, also occurred somewhat by accident.

Picture our early farmer friends and the vessels available in which milk could be stored: the tightly woven reed basket, the earthenware pot, and the repurposed digestive tract of a beast. It turns out that the stomach of many young mammals is the natural source for a very powerful milk coagulant — what we cheesemakers call *rennet*. When such an animal stomach was used as a vessel for fresh milk, the rennet would have *curdled* and thickened the milk while the milk naturally soured, resulting in solid cheese curds and liquid whey. Broken pieces of ancient

The author and a few of the aged cheeses she makes at Pholia Farm Creamery. CREDIT: BRENTON BURK

pottery strainers indicate that cheese curds were being purposefully drained and separated from whey as long as 7,500 years ago. It isn't too big of a leap to conclude that other means of straining curd also existed — maybe even long before someone figured out how to make a clay colander — but did not survive the ravages of time. No matter what means were used, once humans learned the secrets of making curd, cheesemaking became a part of almost every culture that herded, milked, and butchered animals.

THE PEDIGREE OF A CHEESE

Today we have the luxury of buying, eating, and making pretty much any type of cheese we fancy, a privilege unique to our time. We have access to books, recipes, and, even more importantly, technology and supplies. But, it is vital to remember that classic cheese types and varieties evolved due to the innate characteristics and assets of a certain place and time. Cheeses that are heavily salted or stored in salted whey, such as feta, developed in places like Mediterranean Greece, where salt was readily available and other means of preservation, such as cold caves, were not. Delicate surface-ripened French goat's milk cheeses were the most organic and lovely expression of the qualities inherent in the breeds of goats being milked and the circumstances of location. Enormous wheels of hard, nutty, sweet Swiss types gained their flavor from the grasses and herbs that grow during the high Alpine summer, and their size made it possible to maximize transportation of wheels (on the backs of donkeys) down the mountains when winter grew near.

As a cheesemaker, the pedigree of any cheese is something to honor and appreciate. It is also something to keep in mind when you are unable to exactly reproduce your favorite Spanish blue or English cheddar. The qualitiy that a location imparts on cheese (or wine, beer, or coffee beans) is called *terroir* (*tare-WAH*). From the breed of cow, goat, or sheep to what those animals ate and the traditions of the cheesemaker, terroir cannot be cloned. It is what we artisan producers count on when sharing our recipes. We know that no matter what, each finely crafted cheese — when made from the milk of animals nurtured on regionally specific foods — will be a unique expression.

As you learn to make cheese, it is natural and even helpful, to "copy" classic recipes and styles — or at least to attempt to duplicate them. It helps us learn the steps and gives us a frame of reference for our goal. But also it teaches an equally important lesson: the incredible variety of possible outcomes, even when precise steps are followed. Don't let this unpredictability be discouraging. It isn't an exaggeration to say that some of the best cheeses made today came about in good part due to a "mistake" or accidental deviation on the part of the cheesemaker. Maybe one day a century from now, an aspiring cheesemaker will be trying to copy a cheese that you created by happenstance.

WHAT IS CHEESEMAKING?

During most of our history as a species, we have not had refrigeration, so foods were either consumed immediately or preserved in some fashion, usually through salting, drying, or souring — or sometimes, as is the case with cheese, all three. Cheese begins with souring, or fermentation. Then it is "dried" through the removal of the whey, salted, and often dried further through pressing and aging. We'll go over all of the detailed steps in making different categories of cheese later, but let's take a quick look at the preservation techniques used in making cheese.

A few years ago, if you said the word "fermentation," you might have gotten some pretty quizzical looks. Other than its usage by avid beer brewers or winemakers, the word was largely consigned to notions of unwanted spoilage. Happily for all of us that love to make and eat great food, fermentation is now quite the *en vogue* craft. From kombucha (fermented tea) to kimchi and kraut, fermented products are everywhere. Fermentation is simply the eating of sugars by such microscopic life forms as bacteria and yeasts. The by-products of this microbial feast are acid, alcohol, and gas. Fermentation will occur without any help by humans: a tub of beans left in the back of the fridge or a jar of raw milk left on the counter are all wonderful banquets for wild microbes and will ferment if given time, but not necessarily with tasty results

Clean, raw milk will coagulate naturally when the right native milk flora is present. Commercial cheesemaker, Rona Sullivan of Bonnyclabber Cheese on Sullivan's Pond Farm in Eastern Virginia, makes her cheeses the old-fashioned way — with no cooking, starter cultures, or rennet. PHOTO BY AND COURTESY OF RONA SULLIVAN (woe to he who opens that inflated tub of old beans and takes a whiff!). But, with a little guidance and intervention, fermentation can produce wonderful, healthy foods.

In the case of cheese, fermentation takes place thanks to either naturally occurring (wild) bacteria or added (*starter culture*) bacteria that consume the milk sugar and create acid. Not all cheeses are fermented (the lessons in chapter 4 have acid added to the milk), but the vast majority are either partially or fully fermented, meaning that almost no milk sugar (food for the bacteria) remains in the cheese. The acid that results from fermentation protects the cheese for longer storage, helps transform the milk into curd, and adds flavor.

The drying step of cheesemaking is accomplished by naturally coaxing the water out of the curd through draining (as in the Neolithic sieve we mentioned earlier), in some cases by adding weight to press out the moisture, and then often by allowing the cheese to sit or hang for an extended period of time. Fortuitously, these steps in removing water also concentrate nutrients and flavor; allow for the further breakdown of milk sugar; give time for the **proteins** in the milk to break down into more easily digested parts; and create a portable, well preserved, and delicious food.

Salting is an essential step in cheesemaking. Without salt, cheese is bland. Without salt, cheeses do not lose enough moisture and are easily spoiled. Without salt, cheese is not complete.

Bear in mind that there are cheeses with salt, and there are salty cheeses. Those that are traditionally much higher in salt are so because of the traditions involved both in their crafting and in the way they are enjoyed.

To sum it up, cheesemaking is many things: It is natural fermentation and the preservation of food; it is science and art; it is a hobby and a profession; and it is a challenge and a pleasure. Whatever your original motivation was for learning to make cheese, a wonderful journey awaits, one that will teach you many things and provide endless hours of satisfaction — and, of course, delicious cheese!

NOTES

....

2: UNDERSTANDING INGREDIENTS

CHEESE IS ONE OF THE SIMPLEST FOODS ever created by humans. All you really need to make cheese is a bowl of fresh unpasteurized milk and patience. After a number of hours, natural fermentation will create a primitive curd that can be rescued from the whey with a basket or even your hands. While rather bland without the addition of salt, it is still cheese. Much like the tale of stone soup in which a clever vagabond crafts an extravagant feast from water and stones, delicious and complex cheeses can arise from the humble combination of milk and time. To learn to make cheese is to learn to love what milk can become. Let's take a look at all of the necessary ingredients, plus a few optional ones, that go into making cheese in the order that we'll be using them in the recipes.

A QUICK LOOK

Milk: Cheese starts with fresh, raw, or pasteurized whole or partly skimmed milk (never *ultra-pasteurized* [UP] or *ultra-high-temperature* [UHT]), most often from dairy cows, goats, and sheep.

Acid: Many quick cheeses are made using food acids such as vinegar, lemon juice, citric acid, and tartaric acid.

Culture: Most cheeses rely upon acid that is created by starter culture bacteria.

Calcium Chloride: (optional) A mineral solution often added to help *coagulate* the milk.

Lipase: (optional) An animal-source ingredient that creates the sharp, piquant flavor desired in some cheeses. (None of the recipes in this book call for lipase.)

Rennet: An enzyme that helps coagulate the milk. Rennet, as a liquid or tablet, can derive from several sources: plants, microbes, and animals.

Salt: Salt is added to cheese for flavor and preservation. **Pure salt**, without any added ingredients, is the best choice for cheesemaking.

Flavorings: (optional) Herbs, spices, beer, smoke, and a variety of other ingredients can be added to most cheeses for additional flavor.

MILK

From the killer whale to the kangaroo, the guinea pig to humans, all mammals owe their start in life to milk. The first food of this large, diverse group of creatures, nutrient-packed milk is designed to meet all of the needs of their helpless offspring. These nutrients are also what make it possible to convert milk into cheese. Understanding the nuances of milk is the greatest task of every cheesemaker, whether novice or pro.

All great cheese starts with great milk. Here a Jersey cow is being milked into a hooded pail at By George Farm, Applegate, Oregon.

The majority of the world's modern cheeses are made from the milk of domesticated cows, goats, sheep, and water buffalo. At some points around the globe, milk for drinking and fermenting is collected from more exotic beasts such as donkeys, horses, camels, yaks, and even reindeer. As you may imagine, this great variety of milk offers a diverse assortment of cheesemaking possibilities. What you may not know is that even the milk from a single animal will change throughout the year and throughout her life. Unlike the seasonal production of the small farm, the modern, large-scale milk supply is managed in a fashion so as to limit these variations and provide the most consistent milk possible (see sidebar Milk's Journey from the Farm to the Grocery Store). While this might be a desirable quality for the shopper expecting a glass of milk to taste the same all year long, it comes at a price

MILK'S JOURNEY FROM THE FARM TO THE GROCERY

Most grocery store milk goes through several steps of processing before it reaches your local market. Milk is collected at the farm in a large cooling container called a bulk tank. It is usually picked up from the bulk tank approximately every other day by a milk tanker truck. In the truck's large holding tank, it is combined with milk from several other farms and then transported to the processing and bottling facility. While most facilities bottle daily, milk can sit in an even larger holding tank called a milk silo for several more days before being processed. Samples of milk are tested for safety issues, such as disease-causing bacteria, and other factors such as how much fat it contains. From the silo, milk moves through a series of machines. In one it might have the cream removed, such as in the case of skim or low-fat milk. Then it is pumped through a pasteurizer that heats and cools the milk to temperatures stipulated by the Pasteurized Milk Ordinance (PMO), the U.S. Food and Drug Administration's regulatory document on pasteurized milk production. Following pasteurization, most milk is *homogenized* by pushing it through a series of screens that resize the large fat *globules* into tinier pieces that will not float to the top. Before bottling, milk is standardized to the desired fat content — for example, 1% or 2% — and vitamins, destroyed by pasteurization or deemed nutritionally or economically advantageous, are added. Some milk is treated to other processes too, such as microfiltration and ultra-high-temperature pasteurization, which greatly extend its shelf life. (Sadly, most of the organic cow's milk and commercially available goat's milk are ultra-pasteurized.) Once packaged, the milk is crated and transported to the grocery store.

for those hoping to transform the milk into cheese.

The Components of Milk

Milk is mostly water, and indeed making cheese is in large part just the separation of the watery element of milk from its solid constituents: fat, protein, and minerals. Because of the way that these *components* behave in the presence of acid and rennet, it is possible to consolidate the nutritious solids as *curd*, leaving the water and a few other components behind as a translucent liquid called *whey*. Let's take a look at each of the components in milk — sugar, fat, protein, minerals, and vitamins — and see what role they play in the creation of cheese.

Milk sugar, or lactose, serves as food for cheesemaking bacteria, either those naturally in raw milk or those added as a starter. (As we learned in chapter 1, fermenting bacteria metabolize the sugar and produce acid.) The lactose content of milk changes throughout the year, but it does not vary that much between most milking species. Fresh cheeses made from all milks will still have quite a bit of lactose in them, but varieties that age for longer than a month are virtually lactose-free, making them digestible for those who cannot fully digest lactose.

Milk fat is mostly captured in the cheese-making process and lends flavor and texture to the final product. Some cheeses are made using milk that has had some of the fat, as cream, removed. Removing the fat changes the texture of the cheese, but mostly it changes the flavors that develop during aging. Other cheeses have extra cream added, such as cream cheese and triple-cream Brie. The fat in milk varies greatly depending upon the species of the animal, what it eats, and the time of year. For example, goat's milk typically has more types of fat that are known for lending strong, musky flavors and smells under certain conditions. (This is contrary to the old farmer's tale of goat's

The Average Fat and Protein Content of Several Milk Producing Species and Breeds

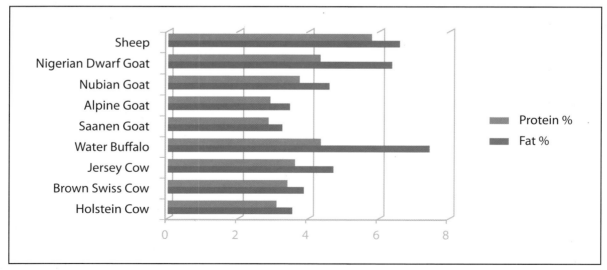

milk being tainted by the proximity of the buck.) Homogenization, over-agitation (from milk pumps used in processing plants), and unwanted microbes all damage milk fat and can lead to unwanted flavors in cheese. Goat's milk, with its smaller, more fragile milk fat globules, is the easiest to damage.

Milk protein comes in several varieties; some are better at making cheese than others, thanks to their structure. It is the *proteins* in milk that knit together to form a network that becomes the cheese curd. During aging, the proteins in cheese are broken down to smaller segments that provide flavor and aroma and are easier to digest. The amount of high-quality cheese protein in milk can vary by breed and species. For example, many goat breeds have far less of the most desirable cheese proteins, making their milk more suitable for fluid use and certain types of cheese. Milk proteins like fat globules can be damaged and altered by *pasteurization*, homogenization, cold storage, and unwanted enzymes from bacteria.

Milk contains several minerals, but the most important one for the cheesemaker to understand is calcium phosphate, which we'll call simply "*calcium*." This mineral is responsible for creating a strong protein network during coagulation. It is also takes credit for much of the final texture of a cheese. Once fresh milk has been refrigerated, the calcium begins to behave differently and becomes less available for helping with coagulation. Even high-quality raw milk that has been refrigerated for 24 hours will experience a change in mineral balance that will affect coagulation. For this reason, a mineral solution of *calcium chloride* is often added to the milk before coagulating. In general, the

WHY THE FAT OF GOAT'S MILK DOESN'T FLOAT

Fat globules in milk are larger and more buoyant compared to the other components. When cow's milk is allowed to sit, the fat rises to the top as cream. The fat in the milk of goats, sheep, and water buffalo does not separate as rapidly because the globules are much smaller and because these milks lack a protein that causes the globules to clump together like a bunch of balloons and rise even faster. The cream in these milks can be separated using a piece of equipment called a cream separator. Varieties from breeds that produce high fat will form a nice natural cream layer after a few days sitting in the refrigerator. In addition, the placing of cooled goat milk in the freezer for a few hours, but not long enough to actually freeze, will speed the rise of cream to the top. Remember these types of milks cannot truly be called "naturally homogenized," rather they simply do not naturally separate quickly.

more calcium that is left in the curd, the more pliable, sliceable, and supple the cheese, while the less calcium that remains, the more crumbly and breakable the texture.

Milk also contains vitamins, but they don't play a major role in cheesemaking. The presence or absence of vitamin A relates to the color of the milk and the resulting cheese. The more yellow color of cow's milk compared to that of goats, sheep, and water buffalo is due to the presence of an organic compound called beta-carotene that exists in plants, particularly orange-colored fruits and vegetables. Our bodies convert beta-carotene into vitamin A. Animals that make milk that does not contain beta-carotene have already converted the beta-carotene they have eaten into vitamin A, thus their milk is whiter.

Choosing and Storing Milk

For the recipes in this book, you can use cow, goat, or sheep milk for any recipe, but be sure to follow the tips below for choosing your milk. Most cheeses are best made with whole, unskimmed milk. Grocery store cow's milk, with the exception of non-homogenized or cream top milk, is neither, as even the highest fat content product has been standardized to a regulated percentage of 3.2–3.5%. If you are using farm-fresh raw milk, the fat percentage will be closer to what is natural for the animal. This percentage depends not just on the type of animal, but also on the breed as different breeds within the same species may have milk with a very different fat content. (At this stage in the cheesemaking game, you really don't need to think too much about the differing fat contents, but it is useful

TIPS FOR CHOOSING AND STORING COMMERCIALLY AVAILABLE MILK

Don't use *ultra-pasteurized* (UP) or *ultra-high-temperature* (UHT) pasteurized milk; the proteins in these types of milk are too damaged and will not form a strong network in the curd. High-temperature pasteurized milk is labeled as such, while lower temperature pasteurized milk will simply say "pasteurized."

When available and affordable, use non-homogenized milk, often called *cream-top* or *cream-line* milk, thanks to the layer of cream that forms as the milk sits. The cream in this type of milk is somewhat changed by pasteurization and is difficult to mix back into the milk once it has separated. But the flavor and texture of cheeses made using cream-top milk will be superior.

Choose the freshest milk possible, and use it as soon as possible. Don't be shy about asking the dairy department manager about when they receive new milk deliveries.

Experiment with different brands and at different times of the year; you might find some work a bit better than others.

TIPS FOR CHOOSING AND STORING UNPROCESSED, UNPASTEURIZED MILK

1. Educate yourself about the standards of production for high-quality milk (see the appendix for more).
2. Follow handling guidelines for raw milk (see appendix).
3. Choose the freshest milk possible, and use the milk as soon as possible. Milk should be no older than four days and ideally less than 24 hours old.
4. When in doubt, milk can be gently heat treated at home (see next sidebar).
5. The U.S. Food and Drug Administration (FDA) currently recommends that raw-milk cheeses be aged for a minimum of 60 days.

HEAT TREATING MILK

There are many occasions when heat treating, or pasteurizing, raw milk is a good idea. Every consumer and user must find their own level of comfort with raw milk on their own, hopefully after researching the topic. Should you decide to heat treat, it can be done simply using the same pot and water-bath setup that you will learn about in chapter 3. There are three levels of heat treatment that are good options for the home cheesemaker:

- 155°F (68°C) for 15 seconds: a gentle heat treatment that is not complete pasteurization, but greatly reduces the number of bacteria in the milk without significantly changing proteins or enzymes (as long as it reaches this temperature fairly quickly and then is cooled quickly. This type of treatment is called *thermization*.
- 145°F (63°C) for 30 minutes: also called low-temperature long-time (LTLT) pasteurization
- 161°F (72°C) for 15 seconds: also called high-temperature short-time (HTST) pasteurization

With any of these methods, you can cool the milk (by setting the pot in a sink of cold water) to the temperature needed at the start of the recipe and then begin making cheese. In our first lessons, in chapter 4, the milk temperatures are all beyond what is needed to pasteurize the milk, so you don't need to perform any of these heat treatments first.

Raw cow's milk with a beautiful cream top, from Runnymeade Farm, Rogue River, Oregon.

In some states, the sale of unpasteurized (raw) milk is allowed, either directly from the farm or in retail stores. If raw milk is of high quality, it can make a superior cheese as compared to its processed peer. But raw milk that has not been collected properly from healthy animals and processed safely can contain disease-causing microbes (*pathogens*) that can cause severe illness, miscarriage, and even death. If you choose to use raw milk, as we do at our farm from our own animals, then you MUST be confident of its quality.

Determining the quality of raw milk, especially from unregulated sources, might be difficult or even impossible for the home cheesemaker. You will have to make up your own mind about your comfort level working with unpasteurized milk, but the tips below will assist you. (See my book *The Small-Scale Dairy* [Chelsea Green Publishing, 2014] for information on producing the best-quality raw milk.)

ACID

In the most basic cheeses, such as those we'll cover in chapter 4, cheese curd is quickly made by adding a food acid, such as lemon juice or vinegar to heated milk.

Choosing and Storing Acid

Any edible acid can be used to coagulate milk. Since the human palate prefers foods that are a bit on the acidic side, there are many options readily available for the cheesemaker. Vinegars, citrus juice, and even wine can be used to coagulate milk — each lending its own characteristics and color. Powdered food acids such as citric, tartaric, and ascorbic can be used when minimal flavor is desired. These granulated dry

to know.) You can make cheese from skim milk, but it will have a rubbery and unpleasant texture in addition to lacking some of the vitamins present in milk fat. Dried, powdered milk can also be used to make cheese, but with similar textural and aesthetic differences. Even if you are limited to only grocery store milk, you can still make some pretty great cheese at home.

acids are also quite convenient to keep on hand due to their indefinite shelf life. Remember, the weaker the acid, the more you will have to use: for example, in order to coagulate a gallon of milk with wine, you might need a bottle or more of wine but only ½ cup (237 ml) of vinegar. Of course, if the wine is no longer palatable and has begun to turn to vinegar, you will need less! Also remember that commercially made vinegars vary in acid content. It is always a good

A BIT ABOUT pH

The pH scale is a way to indicate the presence or lack of acid in a substance. Something that is pH neutral, like pure water, has a pH of 7. As the number drops from neutral, the substance is more acidic. Fresh healthy milk is just slightly acidic, with a pH of about 6.6. (Goat milk on average has a pH that starts a bit lower than cow's milk.) Fresh soft cheeses are usually about pH 4.5, or about as acidic as a glass of wine. Cheeses that are coagulated with rennet and pressed are a bit less acidic at about 5.2, similar to the tartness of a fresh tomato. You don't have to know how to measure pH to get started in cheesemaking, but the concept of acid and how it creates and preserves cheese is important to understand.

Adding vinegar to acidify and coagulate milk.

idea to have a little extra on hand when starting a recipe in case more is needed to get the right results.

CULTURES

Cheese starter cultures contain bacteria and other *microorganisms* that change the sugar in milk into acid and other by-products. When acid is produced by cheese starter bacteria, the resulting cheese will have a much more complex flavor and a potential for developing even more nuanced aroma and character during aging. It is the amount of acid in a cheese, combined with the salt and lack of moisture, that allows it to have a long shelf life — even for years, as is the case for some of the world's greatest cheeses, which can age for a decade.

Fortunately, the cheesemaker today has a tremendous variety of cultures available for purchase (but don't worry, you only need a couple). The home cheesemaker has the additional

RAW MILK AND CHEESEMAKING THEN AND NOW

In the best possible world, milk would be collected from pasture-grazing and housed cows and sheep, and from free-ranging, shrub-browsing goats. During the milking process, the udders would be clean, but not sanitized, and bacteria collected during milking would be mostly harmless, and also helpful to the cheesemaking process. The milk would never be chilled, but would instead be fermented immediately and made into cheese. This idealistic situation is what occurred traditionally when farms were small, multigenerational (meaning plenty of uncomplicated labor), and refrigeration was rare. All of these qualities meant that animals could be managed differently and milk had to be processed immediately — leaving no chance for the growth of unwanted, disease-causing microbes and the best-quality milk — with no change due to refrigeration.

The modern world brings us not only refrigeration, but expanding labor costs, lack of land, and different market pressures that all combine to make the above cheesemaking utopia almost impossible. Most of us seek to find a balance between acknowledging the different realities facing dairy farmers and our desire to make great cheese. For that reason, even the farmer-cheesemaker who collects their own superb quality raw milk is most likely to refrigerate it, add calcium chloride, and use added starter cutlures in addition to appreciating the bacteria and qualities that still raw milk will most certainly bring to the process. Indeed, science and critics all agree that properly-made, raw milk cheeses are more complex and interesting than their pasteurized counterparts.

benefit of several companies that have made the selection process very easy and reliable thanks to the use of premeasured, single-dose packets. While cheese starter cultures are manufactured in several forms, including fresh bulk starter and frozen pellets, the hobbyist will get the best results using freeze-dried culture, often called direct-set, direct-vat set, or direct-inoculation culture.

In the recipes in part 2, I will give measurements for cultures in teaspoons as well as weight in grams. You may notice that the weights of cultures are different than that of the same teaspoon amount for things like salt and citric acid — and sometimes they are even different for two types of culture. Cultures have different densities than things like salt, so the same one half teaspoon of each will have a different weight. For this reason, it is always more accurate to weigh cultures than to measure with a teaspoon, but either way is just fine at this level of study.

Choosing and Storing Cultures

When you first start shopping for cheese cultures, don't be discouraged by the large number of choices (In fact, you can make almost every recipe in this book with only one or two types of culture). Cultures are packaged and labeled for specific cheese types, but there is a great deal of overlap and room for successful experimentation. Most cultures include several strains of bacteria that are intended to produce the right amount of acid as well as provide flavor to the cheese. The many types of starter can be divided into two main groups: *mesophilic* and *thermophilic*. Mesophilic blends grow best in moderate temperatures and are used when making cheeses in which the temperature never exceeds 102°F (39°C). Thermophilic blends prefer high temperatures. As long as you choose a culture from the right group, your cheese-making will be reasonably successful.

Freeze-dried cultures can be stored in a home freezer for extended periods, even years.

Culture Chart

Cheese Type	Culture Type	Gianaclis's Pick	Prepackaged	Quick Substitute
Chèvre, quark, fromage blanc, sour cream	Mesophilic	Flora Danica	Chèvre and crème fraîche starter (includes rennet)	Buttermilk with live active cultures
Yogurt, yogurt cheese, Skyr	Thermophilic	ABY-2C yogurt culture	Creamy and sweet yogurt starter	Yogurt with live active cultures
Kefir, kefir cheese	SCOBY (symbiotic community of bacteria and yeasts) or mother	Live kefir grains (SCOBY)	Kefir starter	Dried kefir grains
Cheddar, Gouda	Mesophilic	MA 4000 series	Mesophilic starter	Buttermilk with live active cultures
Parmesan	Thermophilic	Thermo B	Thermophilic starter	Yogurt with live active cultures

When packaged for use with small batches of about two gallons of milk, they are protected from moisture and contamination. Large packets that contain enough culture for hundreds of gallons of milk can be used in smaller doses, but they can be difficult to protect from problems with humidity and contaminates. My best recommendation for storing larger packets is the use of reusable zipper-lock vacuum-sealable bags. By placing the open culture packet in one of these and removing the air with a vacuum pump, humidity is also removed and the culture will stay very dry.

CALCIUM CHLORIDE

Calcium chloride is a mineral solution that is useful for cheesemakers to have on hand. It is added to the milk to help it to coagulate better and to improve the odds of getting the best cheese *yield* possible. It is also used when making a saltwater solution, or *brine*, in which to soak or store some cheeses, such as feta. Using calcium chloride is always optional, but can be very helpful when using grocery store milk, farm-fresh milk that is over two days old, and often goat milk that is experiencing seasonal variations that affect the coagulation quality.

Choosing and Storing Calcium Chloride

Calcium chloride is usually sold as a dry crystal or diluted liquid. I recommend buying and using the pre-diluted liquid form, as it saves the step of properly measuring and mixing the dry form. Either form can be stored at room temperature for an indefinite period of time; both are harsh in flavor and can cause problems with coagulation if not measured properly. In

chapter 6, I'll tell you how to figure out how much to use and how to add it to the milk.

LIPASE

Lipases are enzymes that break down fats. The breakdown of fat in cheese releases additional flavors and aromas. Lipase is naturally present in raw milk, but is not as strong as the type that is added in cheesemaking. This optional ingredient is added when a *piquant* (spicy, hotness) flavor profile is desired. An example of a cheese with a strong lipase presence is Pecorino Romano.

Choosing and Storing Lipase

The lipase used in cheesemaking is harvested from the digestive tract of a young calf, kid, or lamb — as is traditional rennet. Depending on the animal it comes from, lipase has a different potential for developing flavor, with calf lipase lending the mildest and lamb the strongest flavor. Lipase should be stored in the freezer in the same manner as starter cultures: protected from humidity and other contamination. While I don't call for lipase in any of the recipes in this book, as you progress with your cheesemaking, you may want to try adding very small amounts to recipes such as feta and Parmesan, following the suggestions on the container for how much to add. The resulting products will be distinctively different than those without lipase.

RENNET

The word rennet today refers to several solutions that are added to milk in order to cause it to *coagulate*, or curdle. Rennet contains an enzyme that causes milk to coagulate by changing the way that the proteins in it behave: instead of staying separate, as they do in a glass of milk, the coagulant changes the proteins so that they will stick together. No matter the source of the rennet, whether animal, vegetable, or microbe (see sidebar More about Rennet), they all have a similar effect on milk proteins. The better the coagulation, the stronger the protein network.

MORE ABOUT RENNET

Animal rennet, often called "traditional" rennet, is harvested from the abomasum, or true stomach, of a young calf, kid, or lamb that has not yet ruminated (chewed cud). Before that time, usually when it is less than a week or two old, the baby's stomach contains a high percentage of an enzyme, chymosin, which coagulates the milk it drinks from its mother. This allows time for the milk, now a curd, to be absorbed. If the milk moves too quickly through the young animal's system, the nutrients cannot be utilized. Superior animal rennet should be at least 90% chymosin. Many cheesemakers swear that traditional rennet is superior to all others. I have used both traditional and microbial, and even when used side-by-side on the same aged hard cheese made from the same milk and culture, the differences are extremely subtle, and in blind tastings at our farm, there is an almost equal split in preference, with the slight majority choosing the microbial version.

Junket rennet, found in some grocery stores, is a product made from the fourth stomach of an adult cow and is not a good choice for making cheese as it has very little of the desired enzyme chymosin, but instead contains mostly pepsin, which will coagulate milk, but can also create bitterness.

Vegetarian rennets include those made by microbes (both natural and genetically engineered) and true vegetable rennets. *Microbial rennet* contains an enzyme that is produced naturally by the microbe mucor miehei. It has an undeserved reputation for producing bitterness in cheese, especially hard aged cheeses. It is true that some of the first attempts at the production of this type of coagulant resulted in a product that imparted that unwanted quality to aged cheeses, but brands available now do not when measured accurately. It is my preferred rennet for use in our creamery.

Fermented chymosin is another vegetarian rennet produced by microbes. Unlike the coagulant made naturally by the microbe mucor miehei, fermented chymosin is produced by genetically engineered microbes that have had the gene for producing calf chymosin added to their genes.

True *vegetable-source coagulants* such as those made from cardoon thistle can also cause bitterness. They also are much weaker coagulators and work best with a milk that is high in fat and protein such as sheep's milk. I include instructions for making cardoon thistle rennet in *Mastering Artisan Cheesemaking.*

A strong network helps retain fat in the curd and increase the amount of curd and, therefore, cheese.

Choosing and Storing Rennet

Rennet comes in either liquid or tablet form. Some types are also available in single- and double-strength versions. The liquid form must be stored in the refrigerator and not exposed to light for long. When stored properly, rennet can last up to a year, but may start losing strength earlier. Deciding upon the rennet source — animal or vegetarian — can be a matter of ethics or dietary desires. Most cheesemakers develop their own preference over time. I encourage some experimentation with different types while you perfect your craft. The differences the rennets produce in the cheese will be most evident with aged varieties due to the influence the enzymes have during aging. In our recipes we will be using double-strength liquid vegetarian rennet, which, by the way, can be purchased in an organic version from larger cheesemaking suppliers.

SALT

Salt plays an essential role in cheesemaking, contributing to both the flavor and preservation of the cheese. It accents flavors and prevents a bland, flat taste; it can help prevent cheese from becoming too sour by stopping bacteria from producing more acid; and in aged cheeses, it helps protect them from spoilage by making water unavailable for the activity of spoilage microbes. The right choice for cheese is a simple, *pure salt* that doesn't contain any added minerals, flavors, or anti-caking agents (to prevent clumping). For cheeses that are salted and eaten immediately, the choice of salt isn't as critical. But, for cheeses that will be aged or saved, it is more important to use only pure salt, or sodium chloride.

You will find a rather confusing variety of salt available at the grocery store. There is salt with and without iodine (one of those minerals we don't want in our cheese); canning and canning salt (no additives); kosher salt (may have additives); rock salt (for chilling ice to make ice cream); and sea salt, to name a few. Some are named based on the shape of the salt crystals; for example, *kosher salt* is formed in small flakes to prevent them from rolling off the surface of meat. Kosher salt works great for *dry salting* cheeses, but many brands contain additives. (Diamond Kosher is one that doesn't.) Sea salt, which does not contain additives, comes in different crystal sizes, from fine to coarse. Choose the fine version, as the coarse will not dissolve into the cheese quickly enough. The bottom line is look for a fine or flaked salt without any additives.

We'll be adding salt to cheese both by sprinkling it into the curd, onto the wheel, and by immersing pressed wheels into a salty brine solution. Each method brings different positive qualities to the cheese. Sometimes you can choose the method, but in the beginning it is best to stick to what is recommended.

FLAVORING, COLORING, AND OTHER ADDITIONS

Many things can be added to cheese to add and enhance flavor or to change the visual appeal of the final product. Purists — both those that eat cheese and those that make cheese — might cringe at some of these additions, but many people love them, myself included. When handled correctly, an added flavor should not mask the taste of the cheese, but complement it and add a layer of interest. Similarly, added color, whether on the outside of the cheese, throughout, or in an interior layer, should not be overwhelming or distracting. That said, some very famous traditional cheeses, such as the bright orange French Mimolette, are a bit over the top when it comes to added color.

Annatto is a natural coloring obtained from the seeds of the achiote tree. If you want to experiment with adding a bit of orange color to the inside, or outside, of your cheeses, this is the ingredient you will need. Annatto comes in a liquid form that has a very long shelf life. Follow the instructions on the bottle and remember that very little is needed.

Herbs and spices can be added directly to the cheese curd after it has drained and before it is pressed. Infusions — liquid teas made by simmering herbs, spices, or other additions — are added to the milk before it is coagulated or to the curd after it is drained. Successful combinations with cheese include cumin, hot pepper flakes, fenugreek, fennel seed, caraway, and lavender. Let your creativity be your guide, but be sure to use superior quality seasonings from reputable sources, as contaminants can be introduced.

Ales and other types of beer are also a popular addition to cheese. They are added after the curd is drained, but before it is pressed. The amount is usually no more than about one-tenth of the total volume of milk used in the cheese. Interestingly, beers and ales often pair fantastically with cheeses — often more readily than does wine.

Smoke is an age-old complementary flavor for cheese. While liquid smoke is sometimes added to the milk before coagulation, real smoke provides a far superior taste. Cheeses are smoked either when fresh or after they are aged. Any type of wood chip used to smoke other foods will work, but the smoker must not be too hot, or the cheeses will get oily or even melt.

After simmering hot pepper flakes in water, the liquid is added to the milk just before adding the rennet. The softened pepper flakes are combined with the curd after it is drained.

NOTES

3: THE CHEESEMAKER'S TOOLS

*I*F YOU ARE AN AVID COOK, then you likely have most of the equipment you need to get started making cheese. There are two things to remember about all cheesemaking equipment: First, it should be *non-reactive*, or made from a material that will not react with the acids produced during cheesemaking. (The metals in an aluminum pot, for example, react to acid and will partially dissolve.) High-quality stainless steel is the best choice for most pots and utensils, and food-grade plastic or stainless steel for forms. Second, the equipment should be easily cleaned — no nooks, scratches, or chips that might harbor bacteria and cause safety or quality issues in the cheese.

POTS, VATS, AND CONTAINERS

For heating milk and warming curd, a high-quality, heavy-bottomed, stainless steel pot is ideal. Large pots up to five gallons (20 L) can be purchased from restaurant supply companies. If you are ripening milk at low temperatures, as for a soft, fresh cheese, you can use a food-grade plastic container instead of stainless steel, but in general, stainless is always a better choice as it is easier to clean thoroughly without scratching. Glass jars, such as Mason-type canning jars, with lids are great for ripening and storing cultured milks, which we'll be making in chapter 5.

A *water bath* can be very helpful when warming milk and holding milk at a certain temperature. The water bath consists of the cheesemaking pot being placed in another container that holds water. As the water is heated,

A simple water bath setup for warming milk.

either by the stove or by changing it out from a hot water faucet, the milk warms without any danger of scorching. A water-bath canning pot, designed to heat jars of fruits and preserves that are being canned, with a rack at the bottom works great. Because of their large diameter, these enameled pots, designed for canning high-acid fruits, pickles and sweet preserves, will usually accommodate a five-gallon pot. The rack at the bottom keeps the interior pot from sitting directly on the bottom of the larger pot and allows water to flow around it. A stainless

Thermometers should be checked for accuracy by placing in ice water where it should read 33°F (1°C). This thermometer was reading 10 degrees too high before adjusting the nut on the back with pliers.

steel tabletop warming tray, such as used by caterers, can also make a useful vat for making a water bath. You can also simply place the cheesemaking pot in a sink and run hot water to warm the milk.

THERMOMETERS

Most food thermometers can be used to the monitor temperature during cheesemaking. The instrument should not be breakable (no glass), should be easy to read single-degree temperature changes, and range of temperatures from freezing to boiling. Inexpensive dial types, available at most grocery stores, work quite well. I am not a fan of digital thermometers, as they seem to be more difficult to keep reliable. Be sure to periodically verify that your thermometer is working properly. This can be done by filling a glass with ice and a little water. Immerse the stem of the thermometer into the ice bath and observe the temperature. It should be just above freezing (32°F [0°C]). Most units will have a small nut located behind the dial and around the stem. This nut can be adjusted to correct the reading.

LADLES, SPOONS, AND SPATULAS

Milk and curd can be stirred with any stainless steel spoon, but a flat, perforated cheese ladle works the best, as it allows you to move curd gently without damaging it. It also serves as a way to disperse rennet over the top of the milk and stir top to bottom. A cheese ladle can be purchased from a cheesemaking supply company or you can make one by bending the end of a flat, slotted skimmer (available at most kitchen and restaurant supply stores). A stainless steel and a plastic spatula are also handy for stirring milk at high temperatures and scraping curds from cheesecloth.

RIPENING SPACES

For cultured milks and some cheeses, you will need to be able to hold the milk's temperature for many hours, sometimes up to 24, while the bacteria cultures grow and ripen the milk. You don't need a fancy piece of equipment to do this. You can set up a nice little ripening space using an ice chest, also known as a picnic cooler. Ice chests are simply well-insulated containers and not necessarily just for ice or cooling. If you use an ice chest to ripen your milk, be sure to place a thermometer in the milk so that you can make sure that it stays at the right temperature. If it tends to cool off, you may want to place a jug of water at the target temperature in the chest and cover everything with a towel or two to help keep the temperature stable. You can modify the temperature of the hot-water bottle to help maintain your goal temperature.

Depending on the time of year, you can also ripen your milk anywhere where you can keep it at the right temperature — behind a stove, on the counter, it doesn't matter; as long as the milk is safe from pets, being spilled, or contamination, you can ripen it wherever works.

KNIVES

Curd can be cut with a long, rounded blade knife or a long, rounded spatula such as those designed for putting frosting on cakes. A regular kitchen knife can be used, but may not reach the sides of the pot evenly and is more likely to scratch the surface of the container. Whatever knife you use, the blade should be long enough to reach the bottom of the pot without the handle going into the curd.

You can make your thermometer float by using a small plastic tub with a hole pierced in the bottom.

pH METERS

When you first get started making cheese, don't worry about measuring acid production. As you become a more advanced cheesemaker — or if you are already comfortable with a bit more science — you will want to start measuring acid development as a way to learn more about milk quality and how quickly acid is being made during cheesemaking. This is usually best done using a pH meter. Some folks hope to use pH strips for their cheesemaking, but I don't recommend them as the final word in acid monitoring. While pH strips are helpful at some stages, they are not accurate enough to read the tiny changes that are important to the cheesemaker and can only be used on liquids.

CLOTHS

Cheesecloth is used to collect curd during draining, to help form the cheese during pressing, and also to help the cheese drain well by wicking moisture away from the curd and toward drainage holes in the form. According to the texture of the curd, the cheesecloth needs to be tightly woven so as to prevent bits of curd from escaping through it or being stuck in it. Don't confuse real cheesemaking cheesecloth with another fabric that is also labeled as cheesecloth and is available in many grocery and fabric stores. This type of cloth has a very open weave meant for draining soup stock and jelly; it will not retain the curd of draining cheese. The best cheesecloth has a thread count of 120 threads

Cheesecloth comes in a variety of weaves, some are better for draining one type of cheese or another. Pictured from left, 90 thread count, 120 thread count (my favorite for most cheeses), and organdy (great for draining yogurt and other soft cheeses. Not pictured is a grocery store cheesecloth or gauze which is only about 40–60 thread count and useless for draining cheese.

per inch. Another cheesecloth, often labeled *butter muslin*, with a thread count of 90 threads per inch, might work for some cheeses, but its weave is too open for pressed cheeses.

For extra fine textures during draining, such as yogurt and fromage blanc, a finely woven fabric called *organdy* is a great choice. Organdy can be purchased from most fabric stores. Choose one that is made of polyester, not silk, as it will be much more durable. I am still using the same piece of organdy that I started with in the early 1990s! If you don't have organdy,

a double layer of 120 thread count cheesecloth will work just fine.

Often the lessons call for dampening the cloth before use. This helps keep it in place and starts the cheese draining a bit more quickly. You can dampen the cloth with either warm water or preferably some warm whey from cheesemaking.

FORMS AND MOLDS

Cheese forms, or molds, are usually made from food-grade plastic or stainless steel. Cheese

An assortment of plastic cheese forms. Clockwise from left: Basket form, basket form with straight sides, form with follower, homemade forms, small straight-sided form.

forms need to meet the needs of the cheese — in other words, they need to be sturdy enough for the weight at which the cheese will be pressed and have enough drainage holes to allow the

A stainless steel screw press with pressure gauge.

cheese to drain properly. Some cheeses don't need any weight when being pressed, and others need a great deal. Usually, cheeses that need a lot of weight during pressing don't need as many openings in the cheese form, while those that don't use much if any weight need many openings for the whey to drain from the curd. Forms for cheeses that are pressed should include a follower. The follower is a piece that fits just inside the form and onto which the weight for pressing the cheese is placed. The follower quite literally "follows" the cheese as it presses down into the form.

COLANDERS AND SIEVES

A colander and a stainless steel mesh sieve are useful to help collect curd during the making of many cheeses. Choose a colander that is either made of stainless steel or plastic, not copper or aluminum (for the same reasons that these metals aren't suitable for the cheesemaking pot). I like a small to medium-sized sieve with a finely woven mesh for catching tiny curds.

PRESSES

Very few cheese types need the extreme pressure that a mechanical press provides. Most cheeses can be made by using other weights, such as water jugs or barbells. A cheese only needs as much weight as it takes to press the rind closed and tighten the paste (as the interior of the cheese is called) to the desired texture. If the curd is salted before it goes into the press, as with *cheddar* and some other cheddar types, then the tremendous force of a mechanical press is required in order to get the curd to knit back together. Similarly, curd that is very dry by the

A ratcheting strap press can be made for under $10.00 and will work with any straight-sided cheese form and follower. Pictured here with a large tomme form capable of making an 8 lb (4 kg) cheese.

HOW TO MAKE A SIMPLE, EFFECTIVE PRESS AT HOME

You can make a very effective press for under $10.00 — and without any engineering or DIY savvy! All you need is the following:

1 ratcheting strap from the hardware store
2 plastic cutting boards
1 Cheese form and follower — many different forms will likely work with the same press.

Set your cheese form on top of one of the cutting boards. Set the other board on top. Then connect the ratcheting strap (it should come with instructions) to form a loop. Fit the loop around the sandwiched boards and form and pull the excess strap through the ratchet. Cut off most of the excess, leave enough to allow for larger forms to fit between the boards. Then carefully burn the cut edge of the strap with a lighter so that it melts a little and won't fray out later. There, now you have a press capable of making any cheese! You won't know exactly how much pressure you are applying, but I will give you plenty of tips in the recipes to help you know that you are pressing at the right pressure.

Using a barbell weight to press cheese in a form setting on a rack over a tray. The cloth is covering the follower to help keep the weight from slipping.

end of the process, such as with Parmesan-type cheeses, will likely need a mechanical press. Small screw-type presses that will make about a five-pound wheel of cheese can be purchased from a cheesemaking supply company. They are relatively expensive.

MATS AND RACKS

Mats and racks are needed to set draining and drying cheeses on. They allow for air circulation around the cheese and let any dripping moisture fall away from the cheese. Cheese mats are made of food-grade plastic and look almost identical to plastic cross-stitch mats (available in craft stores). In fact, I know several commercial cheesemakers that use these craft store mats

with no problem. Plastic sushi mats are another nice option. Stainless steel or coated cooling racks (also known as baker's racks) are great to place underneath the plastic cheese mats to help increase drainage and airflow.

TRAYS AND TUBS

During draining and pressing, you may need a tray to collect or divert the whey that is pressed out of the cheese form so that it does not pool around the base of the cheese. A glass baking dish, sink drainboard, or a tray will all work fine for the job. For some cheeses that we will make later, you will need a good-sized plastic food tub with a lid to hold the cheese during brine salting or drying.

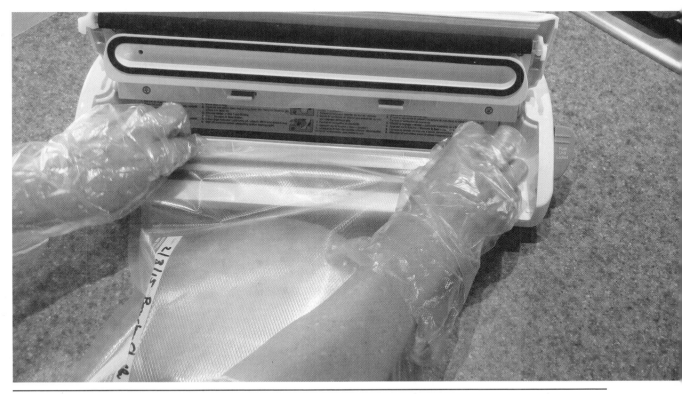

Cheese professional (www.curdsandwine.com) and home cheesemaker Gisela Claassen vacuum seals her original bourbon cheddar. CREDIT: PHOTO BY ARNE CLAASSEN

If you don't mind working with a bit of harmless mold, cheeses can be aged in a plastic tub or a bag to create a natural rind and more distinctive flavor. The tub will help keep the humidity high enough around the cheese so that it doesn't dry out. This method of aging requires quite a bit more vigilance and work on your part than when the cheeses are aged in a vacuum-sealed bag. We'll cover the techniques for aging in more detail in chapter 8.

VACUUM-SEALING EQUIPMENT

A vacuum sealer is handy for storing and aging cheese. Any home-quality vacuum sealer can be used as long as the bags that fit it are large enough to hold your cheese wheels. If possible, choose a sealer that will put a double seal on the bag, or seal it double in two steps. For small wheels, I like to use the resealable zipper-lock type vacuum bags and the handheld vacuum pump that works with them. They have the advantage of being reusable, but the size choices are more limited.

AGING SPACES

Cheeses can be aged at home in the refrigerator or in a wine/beverage cooler. Refrigerator temperatures range from 40°F (4.4°C) to just above freezing at 33°F (0.5°C). Even within the unit, the temperature can vary. All cheeses

A cheese air drying (top right) and others aging vacuum sealed in Canadian cheesemaker Ian Treuer's home aging unit. For more visit www.muchtodoaboutcheese.com. Credit: Photo by and courtesy of Ian Treuer

will age, as long as they aren't freezing, but generally do best between 40°F (4.4°C) and 55°F (12°C). Wine/beverage coolers are designed to keep things at a very cheese-aging-friendly temperature, so if you can get one of these units, your cheeses will thank you. If not, go ahead and use whatever fridge you can — it will still work!

PREPARING CHEESEMAKING TOOLS

The equipment preparation for all cheeses is similar, so we'll cover it just once. I won't include this very repetitive process in the recipes, but you should follow it every time you make cheese.

When I work in our licensed creamery, I use a lot of hot water, a lot of cleaning solutions, and a lot of elbow grease. I also wear scrubs, a hair cover, gloves, and boots that are only used in the creamery. When I make cheese in our home kitchen, I am pretty relaxed by comparison. Cheesemaking equipment should be very clean, of course, but I don't keep a sink filled with bleach and water ready to rinse and re-sanitize all of the tools and my hands.

A thorough handwashing and vigorous scrubbing with dish soap of all of your equipment will remove almost 100 percent of any dirt, residue, or microbes of concern. After each cheesemaking session and wash-up, be sure to allow everything to air dry thoroughly. Bacteria need moisture to grow, so keeping equipment dry between uses is a great way to prevent contamination. An automatic dishwasher can be used to clean equipment instead of hand washing it. Before use, it is a good idea to rewash anything that has not been used and washed in some time, say a week or so. If you are going to use it right away, you don't have to let it air dry.

You can *sanitize* your equipment just before use if desired. For the home cheese kitchen, my favorite sanitizer is boiling hot water. You can fill or partially fill your main cheese pot with water, bring it to a boil, then dip all of your tools into the water. Pour a bit of the water over a tray and lay your tools on this tray. Use the same hot water to rinse your already-clean forms and cheesecloth as well. If you are going to use them immediately, they don't need to air dry.

Part 2:

THE FUN OF MAKING CHEESE

NOTES

4: QUICK AND SIMPLE CHEESES

W'RE GOING TO START OUR JOURNEY by making some really fun, tasty, super simple cheeses. The first lessons in cheese and milk chemistry are also the first dose of the magic of making cheese. In all of the lessons in this chapter, we'll be using heat and added acid to force the solids in the milk — the protein, fat, and minerals — to separate from the watery portion. At the unseen level, milk behaves very differently when it is hot compared to when it is cold. It also reacts radically to having something tangy and acidic added to it — it curdles. The hotter the milk, the less acid is needed to produce this amazing chemical reaction, but — and here's your first important milk chemistry lesson — the hotter the milk when the acid is added, the more chewy the end product will be thanks to the way that the heat changes and helps capture the proteins.

STEPS FOR MAKING QUICK AND SIMPLE CHEESES WITH HEAT AND ADDED ACID

This quick, super easy method involves just three basic steps. It produces a family of versatile fresh dairy products, including such classics as Italian ricotta and Indian paneer. Most recipes in this chapter will yield 1.5–2 pounds of cheese per gallon of milk (0.7–0.9 kg per 4 L) depending on whether the curd is pressed or not.

Heat Milk

This step involves using high heat ranging from 175°F to 220°F (79°C to 100°C) to form curds in the milk. Heat does several things to milk (including destroying bacteria and enzymes), and the changes it causes depend on both the temperature and how long the milk remains at that temperature. For the purpose of making high-heat and acid cheeses, the heat does two helpful things: First, it makes some of the proteins in milk stick together. This makes these cheese types higher in protein and clumpier in texture. Second, the heat helps the acid to coagulate the curd. The higher the heat, the less acid is needed, helping create a cheese that isn't overly sour.

Add Acid

When the milk has reached the goal temperature, acid is added to make the curds separate from the whey. Slowly drizzle the acid into the milk while stirring gently. As soon as the acid is added, all of the proteins in the milk will begin to clump and form curds. (The first time you see this, it is truly amazing.) Continue stirring very gently to avoid breaking the curds up into little pieces; then stop and let the curds and whey set for 5–20 minutes.

Drain Curd

Once the curds and whey have separated in the pot, the curds are drained. This process might

FAQ: WARMING MILK FOR ALL CHEESES

Q: After milking do I have to chill the milk before I make cheese?

A: No. One of the best things you can do if you have access to milk straight out of the animal is to start the cheesemaking or milk fermentation process right away.

Q: How often should I stir the milk while it is warming?

A: That depends on how quickly you are heating it. If it the pot is sitting directly on the hot burner, the milk should be stirred constantly. But, if it is sitting in a sink filled with hot water, you should stir it every few minutes.

Q: If the milk burns a bit, can I still use it to make cheese?

A: In theory, yes, but the flavor will be tainted. It is better to send it to the compost pile or chicken coop and start again.

Q: If the milk gets too warm, what do I do?

A: If the milk gets a little warmer than the goal temperature, you can set the pot in a sink of cool water and stir it until it cools down to the desired temperature. But, if it gets really hot, say about 170°F (77°C), consider making it into yogurt or ricotta, that is, unless you already are!

be as simple as scooping and pouring the steaming curds into a cheesecloth-lined colander, or you might add a step that includes gentle pressing to form a solid cheese. Remember the whey from high-heat cheeses is extremely hot so place the colander over another pot or in the sink to keep from getting splattered.

Store and Use

You can use quick and simple cheeses right away, store in the refrigerator for about a week, or keep in the freezer for many months. Before storing, cover or wrap the cheese tightly in plastic to keep out unwanted flavors and yeasts and

Once acid is added, the milk quickly coagulates into curd, leaving translucent whey.

Acid curd being ladled into a cheesecloth-ined colander.

After a few minutes of draining, you can flip the curd in the cloth if you want to speed up the process.

molds. These cheeses don't have a long shelf life and are prone to spoilage because they are so moist.

WHAT TO DO WITH THE WHEY FROM QUICK AND SIMPLE CHEESES

The cheeses in this chapter will create whey that contains some milk sugar, acid, a bit of fat, and some protein (but not much). There isn't much nutrition in it, especially compared to the whey we'll collect in chapters 7 and 8, so it isn't good for as many uses. You can use it to water acid-loving plants (such as evergreen trees, azaleas, and most berries), pour it in the compost or down the drain, or feed to the chickens.

After draining, paneer curd can be pressed using simple kitchen supplies.

Ricotta three ways, clockwise bottom left: Acidified with cider vinegar, orange juice, and wine.

LESSON 1: WHOLE-MILK RICOTTA

There is a whole family of fresh cheeses made with milk, whey, or a combination of whey and milk to which acid is added. Of these, North Americans may be most familiar with ricotta, but it comes in many other guises around the world including *brocciu* (BRO-shu) from Corsica (made from sheep's whey and milk) and *anari* from Cyprus (made from goat's or sheep's whey and milk). While the fresh versions are better known, the cheeses can be dried and heavily salted to create tangy, pungent grating cheeses. Greek *mizithra* (made from goat's or sheep's whey and milk) and Italian *ricotta salata* are two well-known examples, but gauze bags of traditional *anari* can also be seen hanging in the windows of a few Cypriot cheesemakers. This is your first lesson in cheese anthropology; you will learn as we work together that pretty much every cheese has a doppelganger or two out there. So without further ado, let's make our first cheese!

What You'll Need

Milk: 1 gal. (4 L) whole milk

Acid: ½–⅔ cup (118–158 ml) cider vinegar, or fresh or bottled lemon juice

Salt: Any type of salt, even table salt with added iodine, to taste (here it is merely a flavoring, not a preservative)

Utensils: Pot, spatula, thermometer, ladle, cheesecloth, colander

Process in a Nutshell

Time: 10 min. active, 25–50 min. inactive

Steps: Heat milk, add acid, set, drain, salt, store and use

Step by Step

Heat Milk: Pour the milk into the pot, and place the pot over medium-high heat. Heat the milk, stirring constantly and scraping the bottom of the pot with the spatula, until the temperature reaches 180–185°F (82–85°C). If the milk starts sticking to the bottom of the pot, lower the heat and continue stirring.

Add Acid: Remove the pot from the heat. Slowly drizzle the vinegar or lemon juice into the milk while stirring gently; the curds will begin to separate immediately. Continue stirring gently until the whey is a translucent yellow, about one minute. Watch closely and stop stirring as soon as the whey turns clear.

Set: Let the curds set in the pot, uncovered, for 10 minutes; this gives them time to collect and cool a bit.

Drain: Position colander over another pot or in the sink. Dampen the cheesecloth and line the colander. Carefully ladle most of the curds into the colander, and then gently pour the rest of the curds and whey into the colander. Let the curds drain until they reach the desired texture, 15–30 minutes. (If you want the curds to be soft and moist, drain them for less time. If you want drier curds that are easy to make into a shape, drain longer.)

Salt: Add salt to taste, if desired. (I usually don't add salt since the ricotta is most likely going to be used in a dish with added salt, such as lasagna.)

Store and Use: Use the ricotta right away, or tightly cover and store it in the refrigerator for up to 5 days.

Troubleshooting

Curd is too small or doesn't form: Try stirring more slowly when adding the acid, adding more acid, or increasing the heat.

Cheese is too sour: Try adding less acid the next time and adding it more slowly so that you can see if the curd separates. If it is just too sour to use, try adding a pinch of baking soda to the final product to neutralize the acid.

Recap

Wasn't that easy? Have you tasted it yet? The ricotta will be simple, a bit tangy, and have a pleasant cooked-milk taste. Milk ricotta (we'll learn how to make whey ricotta later) can be made from any type of milk — skim from the grocery store, rich, creamy sheep's milk straight from the pail, even camel milk, should you have one of those lovely beasts around — as long as it's fresh and of high quality. But, the amount of cream or *butterfat* in the milk you select will have a huge influence on the texture of the cheese. For ricotta a certain amount of fat will help make it — brace yourself — creamy, but if you try to make it from something like half-and-half or cream, you will create a very different product. Speaking of cream, let's move on to our next lesson!

Fresh ricotta can be rolled into spheres and used to make these delicious pistachio and nutmeg encrusted balls, drizzled with maple syrup and sprinkled with roasted grapes.

LESSON 2: MASCARPONE

In texture and use, creamy, decadent mascarpone (*mas-car-PŌ-nay*) is more akin to sour cream and crème fraîche than cheese. But, because it is not cultured with bacteria and is partially thickened by draining, it is indeed a member of the cheese family. While the initial thickening process is quick, it takes a day or so of patience to finish the process — but it is well worth it. In the next chapter, we'll be making sour cream and crème fraîche, which you will be able to compare and contrast with this first, thickened cream recipe. These types of spoonable, dense cream are popular all over the world. In Australia there is even a widely available product called "thickened cream" that is made by adding gelatin to cream.

What You'll Need

Cream: 1 qt. (1 L) whipping cream (about 30% fat) or heavy cream (about 36% fat)

Acid: ¼–½ tsp. (1–2.5 g) tartaric or citric acid dissolved in ⅛ cup (30 ml) water

Equipment: Pot, spatula, thermometer, cheesecloth or organdy, colander

Process in a Nutshell

Time: 30 min. active, 16–24 min. inactive

Steps: Heat cream, add acid, drain, chill, store and use

Step by Step

Heat Cream: Pour the cream into the pot, and place the pot over medium-high heat. Heat the milk, stirring constantly and scraping the bottom of the pot with the spatula, until the temperature reaches 195°F (90°C).

Add Acid: Slowly drizzle the dissolved acid into the cream while stirring gently. Maintain the temperature of the cream at 195°F (90°C), stirring gently, for 10 minutes. Remove from the heat and cool to 100°F (38°C).

Drain: Position the colander over another pot and line with a double layer of cheesecloth or a single layer of organdy. Carefully pour the thickened mixture into the colander. Let the mixture drain at a cool room temperature of 65°F–70°F (18°C–21°C), stirring occasionally, until about the thickness of yogurt or sour cream, usually about 16–24 hours.

Chill: Cover and refrigerate the mascarpone until cold; it will continue thickening as it chills.

Store and Use: Store in the refrigerator for up to two weeks.

Troubleshooting

Mascarpone is pretty hard to mess up (other than having the cat find it during the night while it is draining!).

Recap

Now you have two cheeses under your belt. While the process steps are similar, you can really see — and taste — the difference that the thick cream makes compared to the milk. The more fat in the milk, the less clumpy the coagulation will be. You can do more experiments by mixing any proportion of milk to cream, heating it up, and then adding vinegar.

After 16 hours of draining, the mascarpone will be thicker than sour cream. When chilled it will thicken further.

Paneer can be fried and served as a main course or combined with other dishes for protein, flavor, and texture.

LESSON 3: PANEER

If you are at all familiar with Indian food, you might have encountered a firm, non-melting cheese called paneer. A virtual twin to many other cheeses made throughout the world, such as pressed *queso blanco* and Lithuanian white cheese, paneer is — in my opinion — one of the most perfect cheeses. It can be made quickly, it is versatile (since it won't melt), it can be frozen, and it is higher in protein than almost any other cheese (since very little protein is left in the whey thanks to the higher heat used to make it). Making paneer will be your first lesson in pressing cheese, so you are on your way to becoming a pro.

What You'll Need

Milk: 1 gal. (4 L) whole milk

Acid: ½–⅔ cup (118–158 ml) cider or white vinegar, or fresh or bottled lemon juice

Salt: ¼ tsp (1 g) pure salt

Utensils: 1.5–2 gal. (6–8 L) pot, spatula, colander, cheesecloth, 2 plates, heavy skillet

Process in a Nutshell

Time: 20–30 min. active, 1 hr. inactive

Steps: Heat milk, add acid, set, drain, salt and press, store and use

Step by Step

Heat Milk: Pour the milk into the pot, and place the pot over medium-high heat. Heat the milk, stirring constantly with the spatula, until gently boiling, 20–30 minutes.

Add Acid: Remove the pot from the heat. Slowly drizzle the vinegar or lemon juice into the milk while stirring gently; the curds will begin to separate immediately. Continue stirring gently and constantly, until the whey is a translucent yellow, about one minute.

Set: Let the curds set in the pot, uncovered, for 10 minutes; this gives them time to collect and cool.

Drain: Position the colander over another pot or in the sink, dampen the cheesecloth with warm water, and line the colander. Carefully ladle most of the curds into the colander. Gently pour the rest of the curds and whey into the colander. Let the curds drain for 5 minutes.

Salt and Press: Gather the curds up in the cloth and squeeze gently to eliminate any extra whey. Open the cloth and stir in the salt. Gather three corners of the cloth tightly together and as close to the curd ball as possible. Hold the three corners in one hand, and with the other hand take the fourth corner and wrap it snuggly around the other three, as close to the curd as possible. Each wrap of the fourth corner should be below the previous wrap.(See photo) This will create a self-tightening knot called a "stilton knot."

Place the curd bundle onto an inverted plate set inside of a large bowl or in the sink. Place another inverted plate on top of the bundle and set a heavy skillet or other weight on top of the plate; the combined weight should be 3–5 pounds. Press for 1 hour.

Remove the bundle from the press, unwrap the cloth, and — voilà! — your first pressed cheese.

Store and Use: You can use the paneer right away, but if you let it chill overnight, it will be easier to slice. Wrap tightly in plastic wrap or a zipper-lock bag and store in the refrigerator for up to 1 week or in the freezer for several months.

Troubleshooting

Cheese has lots of openings in it and isn't smooth in texture: Use more weight the next time and tie the knot more snugly against the ball of curd.

Recap

Compare the texture of the paneer with that of the ricotta. Even just after draining and before pressing, the paneer's texture should be much chewier and chunkier. The difference in the milk temperature and the time it took to heat to this temperature account for the disparity. The longer milk is held at a high temperature, the more proteins are captured in the curd. Like ricotta, paneer can be made with very high-fat milk, but not with heavy cream. Can you conclude why? Heavy cream has a lot of fat but not much protein. Without a significant amount of protein, you can't make a cheese that you can press and slice.

Paneer, as well as other cheeses (such as those pictured on page 3) can be pressed inside a cheese-cloth bag made by tying a special knot. See instructions on page 54 (under Salt and Press).

NOTES

5: CULTURED MILKS AND CREAMS

Now it's time for us to start playing with microbes, those little microscopic life forms that are responsible for creating every delicious fermented food we eat, from sourdough to sauerkraut. Well, not playing really, but putting them to work for us and with us in our cheese kitchens. Unlike the cheeses in the last chapter — that were rapidly thickened by heating the milk and adding acid — the tasty milk products in this chapter are thickened slowly by the bacteria that make acid. Luckily for us, these bacteria also provide many health benefits and help transform the milk into a grand variety of delicious cheeses, beverages, and spreads.

Cultured, fermented milks and creams occupy the oldest branch of the family tree of cheese; they were created spontaneously whenever fresh milk was left to sit in a vessel at room temperature. Most of these fermented milks were never given unique names or the secrets of how they were made have been lost along with other ancient food ways.

STEPS FOR MAKING CULTURED MILKS AND CREAMS

The processes used in this chapter include the addition of cultures and rennet and a long ripening process. This produces a family of cultures products with two subgroups, depending on the amount of whey in the final product. In this chapter, we'll cover the first group, cultured milks and creams, which retain their entire watery, or whey, portion; they are not drained after the curd is formed the way cheeses are. In contrast, the true cheeses in the next chapter are drained of a good portion of their whey. Most dairy products in this family take several hours to make — but don't worry, you don't have to do much during most of the process! The long ripening process of this method allows for the good bacteria that have been added to the milk to grow and produce acid. The acid eventually thickens the milk into a custard-like curd or a tangy, thickened milk or cream. Drained versions, such as yogurt cheese, will yield about 2–2.5 pounds of cheese per gallon of milk (0.9–1.1 kg per 4 L).

Heat Milk

Milk for many of these recipes is usually only warmed to room temperature, 68–72°F (20–22°C). (The exception is yogurt, which is ripened at a higher temperature of 110–122°F [43–50°C], providing an inviting environment for the desirable yogurt bacteria to grow.) In our last chapter, we heated the milk quickly by setting the pot directly on the burner, but for this chapter's lessons, you may choose to use a double-boiler type setup, setting the pot with the milk onto a larger pot or into a sink filled with hot water to create a warm-water bath. The water will warm the milk gently and evenly.

Add Culture

Once the milk is at its optimum temperature, a small amount of starter culture is added. Sprinkle the culture powder on top of the milk, let sit for a few minutes, and then stir well. This helps prevent the culture from clumping when it is stirred into the milk. Some freeze-dried cultures come in a fine powder and others in tiny pellets. The finer the texture, the more likely clumping will occur. These clumps of culture may never completely dissolve into the milk and, thus, will not help produce acid and may even cause flavor problems in the cheese.

Ripen

In order for the desirable bacteria to grow, the cultured milk must be kept at a specific temperature for a period of time, usually between 4 and 24 hours, depending on the cheese. This time period is called ripening or incubation.

Cultures are sprinkled on top of the warm milk and then allowed to sit and hydrate for a few minutes before being stirred.

Before you make any of the cheeses in this group, you will need to figure out a good place to incubate them. (See chapter 3 for more on ripening spaces.)

Store and Use

Cultured milks and creams will last several weeks in the fridge as long as they aren't exposed to yeasts and molds. They are high in moisture, like the quick and simple cheeses produced in the previous chapter, but since they are packed with good bacteria and are quite acidic, they have a longer shelf life.

WHAT TO DO WITH THE WHEY FROM CULTURED MILKS AND CREAMS

Most of the products you will make in this chapter won't result in any leftover whey, but if you make drained yogurt, yogurt cheese, or kefir cheese, you will end up with some. This whey will be quite acidic and contain some protein and bacteria. Because it is so tart, it isn't the right choice to use for animals, but you can use it to water acid-loving plants (such as evergreen trees, azaleas, and most berries) or pour it on compost or down the drain.

The cultured milk must be kept warm for several hours while coagulation and ripening occur. The pot may be covered, or it might have to be moved to another ripening space where the temperature is stable.

LESSON 4: BUTTERMILK

Ah buttermilk, the tonic for the upset tummy and the secret to fluffy pancakes, but with a name whose original meaning no longer properly describes the product. Today's commonly available buttermilk stole its name from the liquid drained from newly made butter. Raw milk butter, as all butters used to be, contained many good, acid-producing bacteria. After the butter was churned, the extra liquid was pressed from the solids and saved. This true buttermilk was flavorful and slightly tart, thanks to the bacteria, and also contained tiny clumps of butter. When most butter is made today, the milk is pasteurized and the liquid that is removed is bland and has few uses. The buttermilk most Westerners are familiar with is simply milk that has been thickened by flavorful fermentation.

Some of the more ancient fermented milks are still made and enjoyed today. *Koumiss* (also *kumis*) from Central Asia and western China is made from the milk of mares. It is known for being quite tart and having a bit of an alcoholic kick due to the higher sugar content of mare's milk that leads to additional fermentation. In Scandinavia and the Netherlands, milk fermented with bacteria that produce *slime compounds* lends their character to drinks called ropy milks. Modern versions of drinkable milk ferments include cultured buttermilk, acidophilus milk, and Bulgarian buttermilk.

Now let's see what happens when you allow microbes to make the acid that is needed to thicken milk.

What You'll Need

Milk: 2 qt. (2 L) whole to partly skimmed milk

Culture: ¼ tsp. (4 g) Flora Danica, ¼ cup (60 ml) cultured buttermilk from a previous batch, or ¼ cup (60 ml) grocery store buttermilk with live active cultures

Equipment: 1 pot, thermometer, 2 qt. glass jar with lid, spoon

Process in a Nutshell

Time: 15–30 min. active, 8 hr. inactive

Steps: Heat milk, add culture, ripen, chill, store and use

Step by Step

Heat Milk: Pour the milk into the pot, and set the pot into a warm-water bath. Heat the milk until it reaches room temperature, 68–72°F (20–22°C). (You can use it straight from the milking parlor if you like.)

Add Culture: If using, sprinkle the culture on top of the milk, let it set for 3–5 minutes, and stir gently with a spoon for 2–5 minutes. Or, stir in the buttermilk until evenly mixed.

Ripen: Pour into the jar, cover with lid, and let the mixture sit at 72°F (22°C) until slightly thickened about 8–12 hours.

Chill: Refrigerate the buttermilk until cold. It will thicken a bit more as it chills.

Store and Use: Store in the refrigerator for up to 2 weeks.

Troubleshooting

Too tart: Decrease the temperature by 2–5°F (10–13°C) during ripening or decrease the ripening time by 1–2 hours.

Too thin or too sweet: Increase the temperature 2–5°F (10–13°C) or increase the ripening time by 1–2 hours.

Buttermilk is frothy or bubbly: The milk is likely contaminated with yeasts or *coliforms* from contamination during milking; throw it out. If this problem occurs frequently, address milking hygiene and consider heat-treating the milk (see sidebar, chapter 2) for safety's sake and the quality of your products.

Note: The starter culture Flora Danica can produce some effervescence, but I have not seen that happen if the ripening occurs within the time suggested.

Recap

You've made the most basic example of fermented milks: You converted fresh milk that would normally spoil quickly into something that will last much longer, have a pleasing flavor, can be used in untold number of recipes, and make things more tasty and fluffy (think salad dressing and pancakes). In our next lesson, we'll repeat almost the same steps, but with cream, and see how the fat content changes the results.

Fresh, homemade buttermilk is healthy, refreshing, and delicious.

LESSON 5: SOUR CREAM AND CRÈME FRAÎCHE

Before pasteurization became a widespread practice, cream left at room temperature would have fermented spontaneously and naturally just like the fermented milks we covered in the last lesson. These thickened, slightly tart products were used in cooking without necessarily having names. When raw cream became rare, commercially created cultured creams such as sour cream and crème fraîche became popular in recipes and cookbooks. Mexican cuisine has its own version called *crema*, and in Russia you will find a sour cream called *smetana*.

When you first make homemade sour cream, you might be surprised at how different it is from its grocery-store cousin. It is important to remember that commercially produced sour cream is highly processed, often with added thickeners and ingredients, and its fat content is strictly regulated by the government. Crème fraîche, on the other hand, does not have its fat content decided upon by regulators, but rather by the cheesemaker. It is often much richer than sour cream. When it has more fat, it naturally has less protein; this makes it less vulnerable to curdling when added to hot dishes. (Remember from the last chapter that high heat and acid cause milk proteins to clump.) It is therefore a nice alternative to sour cream when adding to hot soups and the like.

What You'll Need

Milk: 2 cups (500 ml) heavy cream (about 36% fat) for crème or light cream (about 20% fat) for sour cream

Culture: ¼ teaspoon (0.8 g) Flora Danica OR 3 tablespoons (90 ml) buttermilk with live active cultures (try using some of the buttermilk you made in lesson 4)

Equipment: Saucepan, thermometer, 1 qt. glass jar with lid

Process in a Nutshell

Time: 15–30 min. active, 12 hr. inactive

Steps: Heat cream, add culture, ripen, chill, store and use

Step by Step

Heat Cream: Pour the cream into the saucepan, and place the pan over medium heat. Heat the cream, stirring constantly, until the temperature reaches 86°F (30°C); remove the pan from the heat.

Add Culture: If using, sprinkle the culture on top of the milk and let it set for 3–5 minutes. Stir gently for 2–5 minutes. Or, stir in the buttermilk until evenly mixed.

Ripen: Pour the mixture into the jar and cover with the lid. Let sit at room temperature, 68–72°F (20–22°C), tasting it periodically, until it has a gravy-like consistency and a tangy taste, usually about 12 hours.

Chill: Cover and refrigerate the cultured cream for 24 hours; it will continue thickening as it chills.

Store and Use: Store in the refrigerator for up to 3 weeks.

Variations

If you prefer your crème fraîche a bit fluffier, simply pour it into a bowl and whisk to thick peaks. You can sweeten or flavor it as well: try adding a touch of maple syrup, honey, or fresh fruit.

Recap

If you have the chance, compare the flavor and texture of the mascarpone from the last chapter with the results of this recipe. They look quite similar and have similar uses, but the method and science behind them are different: high heat and added acid versus low temperature, added culture, and a long ripening time. Now let's move on to a recipe that combines a long ripening of cream with its agitation to force the fat globules to clump.

Crème fraiche can be whipped and used as a surprising and more complex alternative to whipped cream.

LESSON 6: CULTURED BUTTER AND BUTTERMILK

Most of today's butter is made from pasteurized cream with no added culture. But in earlier times, a more flavorful variation was created using high-quality raw cream that contained natural wild bacteria that produced acid and flavor. You can mimic this product today by adding a touch of culture to pasteurized or raw cream. Only a small amount of acid results in the butter, but there is an added layer of flavor and complexity. It can be hard to find good-quality cream in the grocery store; most of it has been ultra-pasteurized and often has added thickeners and sweeteners. You can make butter from this type of processed cream, but if you can get your hands on pure cream, your butter will be remarkably better.

Butter can be churned from any high-fat milk. You don't have to separate out the cream, but doing so will concentrate the fat globules so that they can cluster more easily, and, thus, make your process much more efficient. When slightly cool milk or cream is heavily agitated, the fat globules smash and collide with each other and start clumping. Once the clumping starts, it finishes very rapidly. Then the remaining "butter milk" is drained and rinsed from the clump of butterfat, leaving you with butter.

What You'll Need

Cream: 1 qt. (250 ml) light cream (about 20% fat)

Culture: ⅛ tsp. (1g) Flora Danica or 1 tbsp. (15 ml) cultured buttermilk with live active cultures

Salt: Pure salt to taste

Equipment: 2 qt. glass jar with lid and/or butter churn, spoon, 2 bowls, ice, fine-mesh sieve or organdy (optional), 2 pairs of spoons or butter paddles (Scotch hands)

Process in a Nutshell

Time: 12 hr. inactive, 30 min. active

Steps: Heat cream, add culture, ripen, chill, churn, drain, salt, chill, store and use

Step by Step

Heat Cream: Pour the cream into the jar cover with the lid and let it sit until it warms to room temperature, 68–72°F (20–22°C) Alternately, you can quickly warm the cream in a pan over low heat.

Add Culture: If using, sprinkle the culture on top of the cream, let it set for 3–5 minutes, and stir gently with a spoon for 2–5 minutes. Or stir in the buttermilk until evenly mixed.

Ripen: Cover with the lid and let the cultured cream sit at room temperature, 68–72°F (20–22°C), for 12 hours.

Chill: Place the jar in a bowl or pot of cold tap water and stir the cream until the temperature reaches 50°F (12°C); this will only take a minute or so.

Churn: Pour the cultured cream into the churn or leave it in the jar. Churn or vigorously shake the jar using an up-and-down motion.

After about 5–10 minutes, flecks of butter will become visible on the sides of the jar. Continue shaking until the fat globules cluster, usually just a minute or two more; you will hear a distinctive change in the sound and feel and see an obvious glob of butter forming.

Drain: Pour off the liquid (this is true buttermilk!). If desired, you can strain it through a sieve or a piece of organdy. Rinse the collected butter bits with cold water; this helps remove more buttermilk and encourages the fat to firm up.

Fill 2 bowls with ice and a cup with ice water; place two pair of spoons or paddles in the cup. Empty one of the bowls and transfer the butter to it. Set the bowl with the butter into the bowl with ice. Using a pair of the cold spoons, gently press and work the butter into a ball; pour off any buttermilk as it is pressed from the mass. (Alternate between the pairs of cold spoons to prevent the butter from sticking)

Salt: When the butter reaches the desired consistency and very little moisture remains, stir in salt to taste.

Chill: Press the butter into a tub or form, tightly cover, and place in the refrigerator until completely chilled.

Store and Use: Store in the refrigerator or in the freezer. Use the buttermilk right away or refrigerate for up to 5 days.

Pressing the buttermilk from freshly churned butter.

Troubleshooting

No butter forms: If butter doesn't form and you end up with whipped cream, the cream was too cold.

Butter forms but is greasy and soft: If butter forms but it is too whipped in texture and doesn't separate well, the cream was too warm and churned for too long. Chill the cultured milk a few degrees colder next time, as it will warm up a bit during churning.

Recap

Making cultured butter is a much longer process than making sweet cream butter. It may not be worth the time for each butter-making session, especially if you have a constant supply of cream, but it is worth doing as a way to compare the results and to try making another fermented dairy product. Think about the similarity between this recipe and the one for sour cream; they are almost the same with the exception of churning. It's pretty amazing what a little shaking up will do!

BONUS RECIPE: GHEE

How to make Indian Clarified Butter: Ghee

Ghee made with cultured butter is not only delicious, but allows you to use your homemade butter in place of any oil for cooking — even at high temperatures. The process of making ghee removes all of the water and the milk solids from the butter so that high temperatures do not cause the oil to burn or splatter.

1. Place cultured butter in a heavy bottomed saucepan. Place on low heat and warm the butter at no higher than 110°F (43°C) until it is fully melted, about 5 minutes.

2. Increase the heat a bit until the butter begins to gently simmer. If the milk-solids bubble up, stir the foam back in. Cook on simmer till all the moisture is gone (the sputtering will stop). The butter oil should be golden yellow and you will see milk-solids sunk to the bottom or clinging to the sides of the pan. This will take about 15–20 minutes.

3. Increase heat to medium. During this step (about 30 minutes) the milk-solids will gradually turn light brown. The butter oil will turn yellowish brown. It should not turn dark brown or it will be bitter. As soon as the milk-solids turn a light brown color, turn off the heat.

4. Let it cool slightly and filter the ghee using multi-layered cheese cloth to remove the brown milk-solids.

5. Store in an opaque jar or container at room temperature or in the refrigerator.

LESSON 7: KEFIR AND KEFIR CHEESE

Kefir is distinctive fermented milk — people usually either love it or hate it. A bit bubbly and yeasty, kefir contains an incredible dose of probiotics due to the microbes in the kefir grains. The knobby, gelatinous "grains" are more properly called a SCOBY (symbiotic colony, or community, of bacteria and yeasts). Many kefirs produced commercially resemble thin, drinkable yogurt. Very few of these are made using a fresh, living SCOBY. Once you obtain a kefir SCOBY, it is relatively easy to maintain, but it is a bit of a responsibility (about the level of owning a goldfish). Dehydrated grains can also be used, with more consistent but likely less interesting results.

Kefir (also *keefir* or *kephir*), which originated in the mountains of Georgia in the Caucasus region of Eurasia, is quite likely as ancient as its more well-known kin, yogurt. It is growing in popularity with the recent awareness of the benefits of probiotic bacteria.

What You'll Need

Milk: 1 qt. (1 L) whole to partly skimmed milk

Culture: 2 tbsp. (30 ml) fresh or dehydrated kefir grains

Equipment: Pot, thermometer, 2 qt. Mason-type jar with lid, spoon, fine-mesh sieve

Process in a Nutshell

Time: 24–25 hr.

Steps: Heat milk, add culture, ripen, strain, chill, store and use.

Step by Step

Heat Milk: Pour the milk into the pot, and set the pot directly on the burner on medium low heat. Stir constantly and heat the milk until the temperature reaches 65–85°F (18–29°C).

Add Culture: Spoon the kefir grains into the jar and pour in the warm milk. Screw the lid on the jar and gently swirl the grains around in the milk. Loosen the lid slightly to allow gas to escape.

Ripen: Let the cultured milk sit at room temperature, 68–72°F (20–22°C), tasting it periodically, until it is slightly thickened and a tartness that you find appealing, usually, about 24 hours.

Strain: Position the sieve over another jar. Strain the kefir through the sieve; reserve the fresh grains, if using.

Chill: Cover and refrigerate the kefir until it is cold.

Store and Use: Store in the refrigerator.

Variations

Kefir Cheese: Follow the steps above, but allow the kefir to ripen an additional 24 hours (48 hours total). Position a lined colander over another pot or in the sink. Pour the kefir into the colander and let drain until it stops dripping, about 2–3 hours. Stir in salt to taste. Chill the kefir cheese until it is the texture of cream cheese, about 8 hours. Store in the refrigerator for up to three weeks.

Flavored: Many people flavor kefir to balance the sourness. Fresh fruit, honey, vanilla, and maple syrup are all great additions.

Troubleshooting

Kefir-making is quite forgiving and trouble-free. The main problem is when yeasts from the environment or raw milk contaminate the kefir, leading to an overly yeasty flavor. If the overall flavor is not appealing, try a different source for your SCOBY (they each have their own character) or try using dehydrated grains.

Recap

Think about the similarities and differences between kefir and cultured buttermilk. They might use the same milk and take the same amount of time, but the vastly different microbes involved produce different by-products. Even different kefir grains will impart a different flavor profile to the kefir as will different starter cultures used in buttermilk and cheese. There is a whole world of possibilities just waiting for the opportunity to help you make cheese.

Kefir "grains" are gelatinous clumps of beneficial microbes that sour and flavor the milk.

LESSON 8: YOGURT AND YOGURT CHEESE

I grew up eating lots of yogurt. Our family cow, Buttercup, a beautiful and stately Golden Guernsey, produced buckets of rich milk that my mother crafted into a variety of dairy products. We drained and made what is now called Greek yogurt.

Yogurt (also *yoghurt*) is an ancient food that originated in Central Asia. It evolved in places where the climate promoted the natural growth of microbes that do well in temperatures over 100°F (38°C). This natural process can be helped along by heating the milk to a high temperature, which helps create a thicker product and clears the milk of other competitive bacteria. The heat-loving bacteria that give yogurt its distinctive flavor also have incredible health benefits as probiotics. Yogurt's popularity as a health food began in the early part of the twentieth century and has continued to grow.

Once you get comfortable making yogurt, it takes almost no thought, and you will find that there is great forgiveness and room for deviation in the instructions — especially if you don't mind a variety of outcomes!

What You'll Need

Milk: 1 gal. (4 L) whole to partly skimmed milk

Culture: ¼ cup (60 ml) plain yogurt (choose one whose flavor you particularly enjoy) or ½ tsp. (1.6 g) freeze-dried yogurt culture

Equipment: Pot, spatula, thermometer, bowl, whisk, 1 gal. (4 L) glass jar with lid

Process in a Nutshell

Time: 30 min. active, 4–5 hr. inactive

Steps: Heat milk, chill, add culture, ripen, chill, store and use

Step by Step

Heat Milk: Pour the milk into the pot, and place directly on the burner on medium high heat. Heat, stirring constantly, and scraping the bottom of the pot with the spatula, until the temperature of the milk reaches 185–190°F (85–88°C). (If you want an even thicker, higher-protein yogurt, you can increase the temperature to just below boiling.)

Chill: Remove the pot from the heat and place into a sink. Stir the milk until it cools to 115–125°F (46–52°C) usually about 5 minutes.

Add Culture: If using yogurt, spoon the yogurt into the bowl and add 1 cup (250 ml) of the warm milk, whisk until blended, and pour back into the milk. If using freeze dried yogurt culture, sprinkle directly on top of the milk and whisk until blended.

Ripen: Pour the cultured milk into the jar. Cover with lid and ripen at 110–122°F (43–50°C) for 4–8 hours until thickened and slightly tart.

Chill: Refrigerate the yogurt until cold; it will continue thickening as it chills.

Store and Use: Store in the refrigerator. (The yogurt may grow a bit more tart over time, and the probiotic benefits will decrease as the bacteria die off.)

Variations

Greek-Style Yogurt: Follow the steps above until the yogurt has ripened and set. Position a lined colander over another pot; the colander should sit up away from the bottom of the pot by several inches. Stir the yogurt gently and pour into the colander. Cover with a cloth or lid and let drain, at room temperature, stirring occasionally, until it thickens to the desired

This homemade yogurt is extra-thick naturally, thanks to the creaminess and high protein content of Nigerian Dwarf goat's milk.

texture, about 2–4 hours. Refrigerate until cold. Store in the refrigerator. (Unlike regular yogurt, it will not become much more tart over time.)

Yogurt Cheese: As in the kefir recipe above, yogurt can be drained to a thick, spreadable paste much like cream cheese. Follow the steps above for Greek-style yogurt, but let the yogurt drain until it is about the texture of cream cheese, usually about 4 more hours. A touch of salt added during the beginning of draining will help speed draining and help keep the yogurt from growing more tart.

"Rawgurt": You can also make a yogurt-like cultured product using high-quality raw milk, but out of respect for the long history of yogurt, I would encourage you not to call it by the same name. Follow the steps above but only heat the milk to 115–120°F (46–49°C). This method is likely to make a much thinner, drinkable product almost like a buttermilk-yogurt hybrid. It won't have quite the number of probiotic bacteria as the original because of the competitive growth of the bacteria already present in the raw milk (some of which may be probiotic).

Troubleshooting

Too thin: Some types of milk (especially from some of the large, heavy-milk producing breeds of dairy goats) don't have enough of the right type of protein to make a really thick yogurt. You can try heating it to a higher temperature of 190–200°F (88–93°C) and maintaining it at that temperature for about 15 minutes as a way to help capture more of the whey proteins. Another way to thicken the yogurt — and this is the way that it is done industrially — is by adding thickeners such as powdered milk or

gelatin, but I am not a fan of that approach. If heating it higher doesn't work, I suggest either draining it or considering it a drinkable yogurt.

Too tart: Decrease the ripening time by 30 to 60 minutes and chill it more rapidly by placing in the freezer for an hour or so or in an ice water bath.

Flavor is "cooked": Decrease the temperature of the milk during the heating stage by 5–10°F, but hold it for longer. For example, instead of heating it to 185°F (85°C), heat it to 180°F (82°C) and maintaining it for 15–30 minutes.

Recap

Think about the huge difference in flavor and texture when you compare yogurt to buttermilk. Consider how you used heat to work some of the magic that also occurred when making ricotta (there changing the whey proteins to create curd). You have now learned how to manipulate temperature to both nurture the desired bacteria AND to manipulate the milk chemistry. As you work with different milk types, you can start tweaking your process to adapt to the innate differences in the milk. For example, some goat's milk has a lot of whey protein and not as much cheese protein. It benefits from a longer heating process and higher temperature, so that there is time to change all of the whey proteins and make a thicker curd. You won't always be able to anticipate what you should do with any given milk, but if your yogurt doesn't come out the way you had hoped, you can make some changes during the next batch. Remember, milk is always changing, and the successful cheesemaker must be ready to change too!

NOTES

6: FRESH AND VERSATILE CHEESES

THUS FAR WE HAVE USED TWO METHODS to make products, first a combination of heat and added acid to curdle milk, and second, added starter culture to cause bacteria to produce acid and curdle milk. Now we are ready for the next steps in the process, using a tiny amount of rennet to help coagulate the milk, and draining of the curds. These steps take a while as the added bacteria must be given time to produce enough acid to form a curd. With the addition of a touch of rennet, the milk will achieve a much thicker consistency than any of the products in the last chapter. This is also the first time that calcium chloride is used in the recipes, since it is only helpful if you are using rennet. All of the cheeses that we will make in this chapter are tender, soft, and meant to be used fresh.

As with the other cheese and milk products we have made so far, there is a huge variety made throughout the world that go by many different names — so many, in fact, that I could make this chapter about four times longer. But you wouldn't learn any more, other than that there is little difference between these recipes.

STEPS FOR MAKING FRESH AND VERSATILE CHEESES

The method for making fresh and versatile cheeses is essentially the same as the one for making cultured milks and creams (see Steps for Making Cultured Milks and Creams, chapter 5, pages 57–59) only with a few additional steps after the milk is heated and the culture is added. This method yields about 2–2.5 pounds of cheese per gallon of milk (0.9–1.1 kg per 4 L), depending on how long it the cheese is drained.

Follow the steps for heating the milk and adding the culture, then continue with the following steps:

Add Calcium Chloride

If calcium chloride is to be used (it is usually optional, but sometimes helpful), it is always diluted and added at least 5 minutes before the rennet; it is never added afterwards or the coagulation will be erratic and broken. The recommended dose of calcium chloride is approximately equal to the amount of single-strength rennet used, or about ⅛ tsp. (0.7 ml) per gallon of milk. It should be diluted in cool tap water before it is added to the milk. Use ⅛ cup (30 ml) water for every ⅛ teaspoon (0.7 ml) of calcium chloride.

Add Rennet

Before adding rennet, it should be measured very carefully; too little will not provide enough enzymes to properly coagulate the milk, and too much will add odd flavors and bitterness. All rennet types must be diluted or dissolved

Diluted rennet is added by pouring it over a slotted utensil so that it disperses evenly across the milk and can be stirred efficiently.

in cool, non-chlorinated water before adding to the milk. If only chlorinated water is available, it can be easily dechlorinated by adding a drop or two of milk, just enough to add a touch of milkiness. (The presence of the milk inactivates the chlorine.)

Before adding the rennet, start stirring the milk using an up-and-down motion with a ladle or spoon; this gets the milk moving so that the rennet mixes in as quickly as possible. Stop stirring briefly and pour the diluted rennet over the flat part of the ladle so that it splatters across the surface of the milk, and then continue stirring with that up-and-down motion for about ten strokes. Hold the flat part of the ladle to the top of the milk in several spots to help still the milk. As soon as the rennet is added, it starts doing its invisible work. By stirring well, but not in a swirling motion, you are able to mix it in thoroughly and get it to stop moving quickly. This helps ensure that it coagulates as evenly as possible.

Ripen and Coagulate

After the rennet has been added, the milk must sit very still and not be bumped or stirred. Even vibrations from a counter or floor can cause tiny breaks in the coagulation. The coagulation period will usually last about 20–60 minutes, depending on the type of cheese.

Drain

Once the curd has thickened to the desired texture and tanginess, some of the whey is removed by draining the curd in a bag, cloth or form. These cheeses are too soft and mushy to be pressed or drained in a loosely woven cloth, so you must use a fabric that is fairly tightly woven. The bag or cloth is usually hung or suspended in some manner allowing gravity to do the work of whey removal; the handle of a ladle, or other sturdy utensil, set across a pot works nicely for this. Once the desired texture is achieved, the curd is stirred, salted, and refrigerated — or devoured!

Store and Use

Cultured fresh cheeses will last several weeks in the fridge as long as they aren't exposed to yeasts and molds. They are high in moisture, like the quick and simple cheeses produced in chapter 4, but lower in moisture than the cultured milks and cream of chapter 5. Since they are loaded with good bacteria and are quite acidic, they have a long shelf life, and some can even be frozen with very little change in texture upon thawing.

WHAT TO DO WITH THE WHEY FROM FRESH AND VERSATILE CHEESES

The cheeses in this chapter will create whey that contains some milk sugar, acid, a bit of fat, and some protein. There isn't much nutrition in it, especially compared to the whey we'll collect in chapters 7 and 8, so it isn't good for as many uses. You can use it to water acid-loving plants (such as evergreen trees, azaleas, and most berries), or pour it on compost or down the drain.

When the milk has fully coagulated and ripened, it will pull away from the sides of the pot and a thin layer of whey will cover the surface.

Chèvre or fromage blanc curds can be hung to drain over a pot.

LESSON 9: QUARK, CHÈVRE, AND FROMAGE BLANC

These are examples of three cheeses by different names that are all made by the same method. All of them involve the same precise steps, but each is made with different milk. Quark (from Germany) and *fromage blanc* (from France) are both made with cow's milk, but quark is traditionally made with lower-fat or skimmed milk. Chèvre (chev-ruh) literally means goat, but in the United States, it has come to mean fresh goat's milk cheese. Don't be fooled by diverse recipes and a variety of prepackaged starter cultures labeled for each; they can all be used interchangeably. Most of the prepackaged cultures for these cheeses include the rennet in the culture powder, but since my goal in this chapter is to teach you how to use rennet, we will be mixing ours in separately. I always advise starting this type of cheese in the evening so it will be ready to drain in the morning and finished by midday. If you are a night owl and don't mind tending the cheese around midnight, go ahead and start it in the morning.

What You'll Need

Milk: 1 gal. (4 L) whole milk

Culture: ⅛ tsp. (0.2 g) Flora Danica

Calcium Chloride (optional): ⅛ tsp. (0.7 ml) calcium chloride diluted in ⅛ cup (30 ml) cool water

Rennet: 2 drops (0.1 ml) double-strength vegetarian rennet diluted in ⅛ cup (30 ml) cool, non-chlorinated water

Salt: ¼–½ tsp. (1.5–3 g) pure salt

Equipment: Pot, thermometer, ladle, cheesecloth or organdy fabric, colander, spatula, bowl

Process in a Nutshell

Time: 30 min. active, 16 hr. inactive

Steps: Heat milk, add culture, add calcium chloride (if using), add rennet, ripen and coagulate, drain, salt, store and use

Step by Step

Heat Milk: Pour the milk into the pot, and place the pot over medium-low heat or over another pot of water on the stovetop. Heat the milk until the temperature reaches 86°F (30°C). Remove from heat.

Add Culture: Sprinkle the culture on top of the milk and let it set for 3–5 minutes. Using the ladle, stir gently for 2–5 minutes.

Add Calcium Chloride (optional): Stir in the diluted calcium chloride, if using, and let set for 5 minutes.

Add Rennet: Stir the milk using an up-and-down motion with the ladle. Stop stirring briefly and pour the diluted rennet over the top of the ladle. Begin stirring again for 1 minute. Hold the ladle to the top of the milk in several spots to help still the milk.

Ripen and Coagulate: Let the mixture sit at room temperature, 68°F–72°F (20°C–22°C), until the curd is just pulling away from the sides of the pot and the top of the curd is covered with about ½ inch of whey, about 12 hours.

Cut and Drain Curd: Cut the curd into ½-inch (1.3 cm) vertical columns. Line the colander with a double layer of cheesecloth or a single layer of organdy. Position the lined colander or draining bag over another pot. Carefully ladle most of the curds from the pot into the colander or a draining bag. Gently pour the rest of the curds and whey into the colander or bag. Tie the corners of the cheesecloth together and hang from handle of the ladle and set across the top of the pot. Allow the curds to drain at room temperature, 68°F–72°F (20°C–22°C), until the desired texture is achieved, 4–6 hours. (Drain for longer in a cooler room or shorter in warmer room.)

Salt: Using the spatula, scrape the cheese into the bowl. Add ¼ tsp. salt and stir gently but thoroughly until the salt is dissolved and dispersed. Taste and add the remaining salt, if desired. You can use the cheese right away, but it will improve in flavor if allowed to chill for a day or two.

Store and Use: Tightly cover and store in the refrigerator for up to 3 weeks or in the freezer for up to 8 months.

Soft, fresh cheeses can be layered along with ingredients such as herbs, nuts, and dried tomatoes to make crowd-pleasing tortas. This one was made using fresh goat's milk cheese made at Crush Pad Creamery in Oregon.

Shaped cheeses: To form the cheese into logs or rounds, the curd can be partly drained in a bag, salted, and then spooned into well-perforated basket forms and drained overnight. Alternatively, the shapes can be salted after draining. Formed cheeses can be sprinkled with herbs, spices, and so on. They can also be formed in layers, with seasonings and other ingredients alternating with layers of cheese. These are often marketed as "tortas" here in the United States.

Troubleshooting

Bubbly, frothy curd: This is called early blowing and is a sign of contamination by coliform bacteria. Coliforms are from the environment and can be harmless, but may also include some extremely dangerous, disease-causing germs. They can contaminate raw milk or be introduced into pasteurized milk after it is heat treated. Throw the batch out and review your equipment sanitation. If you are using raw milk, consider choosing a different source (see chapter 2).

Too sour: The curd fermented too quickly and became too acidic. Try lowering the ripening temperature by a few degrees and/or adding less starter culture.

Not tangy enough: Let the curd ripen for an hour or so longer or raise the ripening temperature by a few degrees.

Off or odd taste: The milk contained bacteria or yeasts that caused unwanted fermentation during ripening. Consider a different source of milk or try pasteurizing if the milk is raw. Milk can also get off flavors from the overzealous use of cleaners and chemicals such as bleach that leave an unseen residue on surfaces that taints the milk.

Not thick enough: Try adding an additional drop of rennet and add calcium chloride if you haven't already.

Recap

Compare this cheese to our cultured buttermilk from the last chapter. The cultures, ripening temperature, and time are all the same, but the tiny bit of rennet used in this lesson caused a stronger curd to form that made this product capable of being drained. If you tried to drain buttermilk, it would go right through the cheesecloth. Yogurt can be drained because of the higher milk temperature that helps the proteins clump together better. Kefir cheese will drain because it is allowed to become extremely acidic, which leads to a heavier curd. Now let's see how a big difference in milk fat changes the same type of recipe — not unlike what we did when comparing ricotta to mascarpone and buttermilk to crème fraîche.

Soft fresh cheeses lend themselves to many flavor and presentation possibilities including this lavender chèvre by Mama Terra Micro Creamery in Oregon.

LESSON 10: CREAM CHEESE

Cream cheese has become ubiquitous on American grocery store shelves. Foil-wrapped — industrial-produced cream cheese and its slightly lower-fat cousin Neufchâtel (which by no means resembles the soft ripened French cheese with the same name) are staples for use on bagels, in dips, and to make celery sticks a bit more appealing. Homemade cream cheese is quite a bit different. When made with grass-fed cow's milk, the gorgeous yellow color will remind you more of butter than of the Philadelphia brand. It is slightly more of a challenge to make this cheese with goat's milk since goat's milk cream is pretty hard to come by, but you can try using a combination of goat's milk and cow's cream with great results.

In the United States, cream cheese (like many cheeses listed and described by the FDA) has set levels of fat and moisture. The main difference between cream cheese and Neufchâtel is that cream cheese must be at least 33% fat while Neufchâtel must be 20–32% fat. While these cheeses are definitely not the kind to pair with any wine of note, they are useful and desirable in many kitchens. As we learned in the last chapter, this recipe shows again how extra fat changes what happens during cheesemaking. It is an important lesson in your cheesemaking progression.

What You'll Need

Cream: 2 qt. (2 L) half-and-half or light cream (12–20% fat)

Culture: $1/16$ tsp. (0.1 g) Flora Danica

Rennet: 1 tbsp. (15 ml) of this mixture: 1 drop (0.05 ml) double-strength vegetarian rennet in ⅛ cup (30 ml) cool, non-chlorinated water

Salt: ¼ tsp (1.5 g) pure salt

Equipment: Pot with lid, thermometer, ladle, cheesecloth or organdy, spatuala, colander, bowl.

Process in a Nutshell

Time: 30 min. active, 16–28 hr. inactive

Steps: Heat cream, add culture, add rennet, ripen and coagulate, drain, salt, store and use

Step by Step

Heat Cream: Pour the cream into a pot, and set the pot into a warm-water bath or directly on the burner at low heat. Warm the cream until it reaches room temperature, 68°F–72°F (20°C–22°C). Remove from the heat.

Add Culture: Sprinkle the culture on top of the milk and let it set for 3–5 minutes. Using the ladle, stir gently for 1 minute.

Add Rennet: Stir the milk using an up-and-down motion with the ladle. Stop stirring briefly and pour the diluted rennet over the top of the ladle. Begin stirring again for one minute. Hold the ladle to the top of the milk in several spots to help still the milk. (If you are using a fresh non-homogenized cream and milk, don't add the rennet now or the cream will separate before the coagulation occurs. Wait 2–3 hours after the culture is added. You may need to adjust this time depending on how much cream to milk is in the mixture. Try to add it just before the mixture starts to thicken from the starter culture.)

Ripen and Coagulate: Let the mixture sit at room temperature, 68°F–72°F (20°C–22°C), until the curd is just pulling away from the sides of the pot, 12–24 hours.

Drain: Position the lined colander over the sink or another pot. Carefully ladle most of the curds from the pot into the colander. Gently pour the rest of the curds and whey into the colander. Tie the corners of the cloth together and tie the bundle to the handle of the ladle. Set the ladle across the top of the pot. Cover the pot with the lid to keep it warm. Every 2–3 hours, place the bundle in the bowl, open it up, and scrape the thickened sides so that they recombine a bit and don't block drainage. After 12 hours, it should be the texture of thick pudding, if not, continue draining until the cheese is the desired texture.

Salt: Using the spatula, scrape the cheese into the bowl and stir in the salt.

Store and Use: Use the cream cheese right away, or tightly cover and store in the refrigerator.

Troubleshooting

See Troubleshooting Lesson 9, page 78.

Recap

You might recall that our first two recipe chapters were great examples of how differently cream, high-fat milk, and low-fat milk coagulate. The more protein in the milk, the more texture you get in the curd. This same science applies to the comparison of the quark and the cream cheese recipes. If you have the results on hand, compare their textures side by side. The more fat present in the milk, the creamier the results. You could never slice a full-fat cream cheese, at least not cleanly, while a well-drained chèvre log is sliceable. Now that you know this, you can manipulate any of these types of recipes to the desired outcome and you can anticipate the results based on your knowledge of the fat content of the milk — there are no rules! And, remember, it doesn't matter what you call the final cheese, be it Bob's Best or Siri's Spreadable.

Homemade cream cheese — always great on a bagel!

LESSON 11: CURD COTTAGE CHEESE

Now you are ready for another set of skills (notice I didn't say another layer of difficulty). Most of us equate curd cottage cheese — either small-curd or large-curd — as a dieter's option on menus and a common salad bar choice. We think of it as industrial and inexpensive. The making of cottage cheese, however, is fairly time-consuming, and when made at home, surprisingly will not be so different than the mass-produced kind. I have always been a fan of cottage cheese — I love its simple creamy consistency and tender texture.

The term "cottage cheese" is rather undefined. It originated from the fact that it is easy to make over a few hours while other house chores are also being performed, and so perfect for the farm cottage wife and dairymaid. In the old days, fresh, warm raw milk with a touch of added rennet would have been allowed to sour or ripen for a few hours before the rest of the steps of cutting, stirring, and heating were performed. If you look up cottage cheese recipes, you will most likely find that the majority of them more closely resemble well-drained ricotta with added cream. This recipe, on the other hand, is closer to a European-style cottage cheese, which is also made from naturally soured milk, but instead of adding rennet and stirring, the ripened milk is heated until it curdled (shades of chapter 4).

So just what is this next set of skills you are about to learn? The first is cutting and stirring the curd while heating it, and the second is patience at the vat. This, and most of the recipes that follow, require the cheesemaker to stay put and stir the curd for periods of time ranging from 30 to 60 minutes. For this recipe, I will give you two options: one that allows you to step away for a bit but takes longer, and a quicker method that requires you to stay and stir.

What You'll Need

Milk: 1 gal. (4 L) whole to partly skimmed milk

Culture: ¼ tsp. (0.2 g) Flora Danica

Calcium Chloride (optional): ⅛ tsp. (0.7 ml) calcium chloride diluted in ⅛ cup (30 ml) cool water

Rennet: 5 drops (0.25 ml) double-strength vegetarian rennet diluted in ⅛ cup (30 ml) cool, non-chlorinated water

Salt: ¼ tsp. (1.5 g) pure salt

Cream or Buttermilk (optional): 2 tbsp. (60 ml) heavy cream (about 36% fat) or buttermilk

Equipment: Pot with lid, thermometer, ladle, cheesecloth, colander, bowl

Process in a Nutshell

Time: 2–3 hr. active, 2 hr. 30 min.–4 hr. 30 min. inactive

Steps: Heat milk, add culture, add calcium chloride (if using), add rennet, ripen and coagulate, cut curd, heat and stir curd, rinse and drain curd, store and use

Step by step

Heat Milk: Pour the milk into the pot, and place the pot over another pot of water on the stovetop or place pot directly on low heat. Heat the milk until the temperature reaches 86°F (30°C). Remove from heat.

Add Culture: Sprinkle the culture on top of milk and let set for 3–5 minutes. Using the ladle, stir gently for 2–5 minutes.

Add Calcium Chloride (optional): Stir in the diluted calcium chloride, if using, and let set for 5 minutes.

Add Rennet: Stir the milk using an up-and-down motion with the ladle. Stop stirring briefly and pour the diluted rennet over the top of the ladle. Begin stirring again for 1 minute. Hold the ladle to the top of the milk in several spots to help still the milk.

Ripen and Coagulate: Cover the pot with the lid and maintain the temperature of the milk at 86°F (30°C) until the curd is just pulling away from the sides of the pot, 2–4 hours.

Cut Curd: Cut the curd into ½-inch (13 mm) cubes, and let rest at 86°F (30°C) for 10 minutes.

Fresh homemade cottage cheese and summer fruits.

Heat and Stir Curd: Heat the curds very gradually, stirring very gently, to 115°F (46°C) over 60 minutes until they are springy but still tender; increase the temperature a bit more slowly in the beginning. If the curds are too fragile and start breaking when you stir them, shake the pot gently instead of stirring until they are firm enough to stir. Remove the pot from the heat and let the curds settle in the pot for 5 minutes.

THE INTERMITTENT METHOD

If you can't stir continuously for 60 minutes, try this approach: over 90 minutes, raise the temperature in 2–3 degree increments while stirring. Cover and let rest for 5 minutes as each temperature increment is reached. Repeat this step until the goal temperature of 115°F (46°C) is reached and the curds are springy but tender. Continue with remaining steps.

Rinse and Drain Curd: Pour off the excess whey and add cool water to the pot. Rinse and drain the curds four times with cold water. Pour the curds into the lined colander. Stir in ⅛ tsp. of the salt. Let drain for 30 minutes. Taste and add the remaining ⅛ tsp. salt, if desired.

Store and Use: Dress with the heavy cream or buttermilk, if desired. Tightly cover and store in the refrigerator for up to 2 weeks.

Recap

Think about the amount of rennet you used in this recipe compared to the quark and cream cheese recipes. The combination of more culture, more rennet, and a bit higher ripening temperature is what made the milk coagulate in only a couple of hours as compared to the 12 hours needed to coagulate the quark recipe. The quark-type cheese relies on much more acid to help with the coagulation than does the cottage cheese. If we let the cottage cheese ripen for 12 hours, we would have a really grainy soft cheese that we could never make into tender curds. Now you have learned a third important tenet: that the final texture of any cheese relies on the combination of culture amount, rennet amount, temperature of ripening, and time. Don't forget this lesson, because in the next chapter we are going to take everything up another notch.

7: RENNET-COAGULATED SEMI-FIRM FRESH CHEESES

*I*N OUR LAST CHAPTER, we introduced a bit of rennet to help create our cheeses. Now we'll move on to the largest family of cheeses — those that rely completely on rennet for coagulation. Most still use bacteria, too, to produce acid, but the acid alone doesn't cause the coagulation. Because these types of cheese coagulate before they get too sour, the final texture is much more pliable and sliceable, not crumbly and brittle. They also are less tart, able to age for long periods of time, and generally have more potential for complex flavor and aroma development.

At the end of the last chapter, I told you that you are now going to need to apply some principles to your process — namely that every cheese relies upon a combination of time (during ripening, stirring, and draining); temperature (during ripening, stirring, and draining); and final acid content to create the final product. Fresh soft cheeses are quite forgiving if you deviate a bit from the recipe steps, but cheeses that rely on rennet alone are a bit pickier. This chapter will give you practice paying attention to the nuances of these steps. It contains three recipes for three very different cheeses — quick mozzarella (the only one in this chapter that does not use any starter culture), feta, and a farmhouse-type cheese — you can master quickly and begin to feel more confident about your cheesemaking skills.

STEPS FOR MAKING RENNET-COAGULATED FRESH CHEESES

The cheeses in this chapter are a great transition from soft fresh varieties to the more complex cheeses that rely completely on rennet for their coagulation. Many of these are still used fresh, but are obviously great for different types of uses than their spreadable cousins. The last recipe in this chapter can even be transitioned into an aged version. If you are chomping at the bit to make some aged cheese, don't worry, we'll get to that very soon! The cheeses in this chapter will usually yield about 0.85–1.1 pounds per gallon of milk (0.4–0.5 kg per 4 L), depending on how what type of milk is used and how they are drained.

Heat Milk

As with the other methods, the first step is getting the milk to the right temperature. This temperature will vary a bit depending upon the type of cheese being made, but it is typically right around 90°F (32°C). As in the previous method, a double-boiler-type setup, with the pot of milk set onto a larger pot or into a sink filled with hot water, works best.

Add Culture

As in the previous method, bacteria cultures are added to the milk once it has been warmed to the ideal temperature at which they grow.

Sprinkle the culture on the top of the warm milk and allow it to sit for a few minutes while it soaks up a bit of milk.

Ripen

During the ripening or incubation phase, the cultured milk must be held at the ideal temperature for a short period of time, usually 20–60 minutes. It is fairly easy to ripen the milk using the same double-boiler approach you used to warm it. Typically, covering the pot with a lid is enough to keep the milk warm for that period of time. It is a good idea to stir the milk at least once and double-check that the temperature hasn't dropped. If it has, the milk should be gently rewarmed.

Add Calcium Chloride

As in the previous method, if calcium chloride is to be used, it is diluted and added at least 5 minutes before the rennet.

Add Rennet

As in the previous method, after carefully measuring the rennet, dilute or dissolve it in cool, non-chlorinated water. Before adding it to the milk, stir the milk using an up-and-down motion with a ladle or spoon. Stop stirring briefly and pour the diluted rennet over the top of the ladle, and then continue stirring for about 1 minute. Then hold the ladle to the top of the milk in several spots to help still the milk.

Coagulate

After the rennet has been added, the milk must sit very still and not be bumped or stirred. Even vibrations from a counter or floor can cause tiny breaks in the coagulation. The coagulation period will usually last 30–60 minutes, depending on the type of cheese, the temperature and acid level of the milk.

Check for Clean Break

This is really a sub-step of coagulation, but it is one of those steps that sounds so mysterious and brings about so many questions that I want to give it a full explanation. The curd is ready for the next step when it has formed a mass that

---

FAQ: RENNET AND COAGULATION

Q: If the milk isn't coagulating, what are the likely reasons and should I add more rennet?

A: Milk may not coagulate well for several reasons: The rennet may be too old; the water used to dilute the rennet may be too high in minerals, the wrong pH or have chlorine in it; the milk may be low in minerals or high in damaging enzymes; or the milk may be too cool.

Q: If the milk cools down during coagulation, should I reheat it?

A: No, not until after the curd is cut. If you try to rewarm it, you will heat up the curd around the outside of the pot — the heat won't transfer evenly to the center. The outside curds will likely get too warm.

can be cut with minimal loss of milk fat (the large fat globules trapped in the curd can leak out during cutting and stirring). You can check for this by doing the clean-break test: Make a small cut (about 2 inches [5 cm] long and 1 inch [2.2 cm] deep) in the mass with your curd knife, slip the knife, with the flat side up, about 4 inches (10 cm) under the slit in front of it at about a 30-degree angle. Gently and slowly, lift about ½ inch up. The pressure of the knife will cause the cut to travel forward in the curd. If the break is smooth and clean, and the whey that leaks out from the break is not whitish, then a *clean break* has been achieved. If the break is not clean, wait about 5 more minutes then try again. Different milk types and cheese recipes will create a different thickness and heaviness in the coagulated mass, but you will still look for the same result in the clean break.

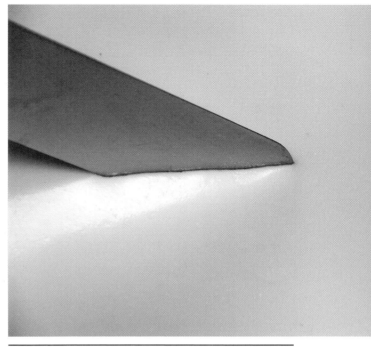

To check for a clean break, first cut a slit in the curd.

Then insert the knife under and forward of the slit and gently lift straight up.

Cut Curd

Once coagulation is complete, the mass is cut into smaller pieces called curds. (No, these are not the same thing as fresh squeaky cheese

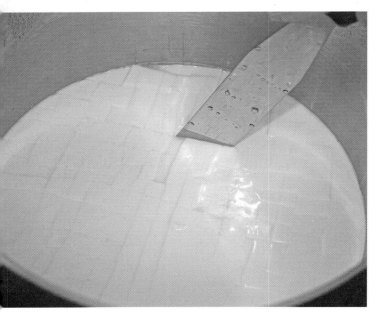

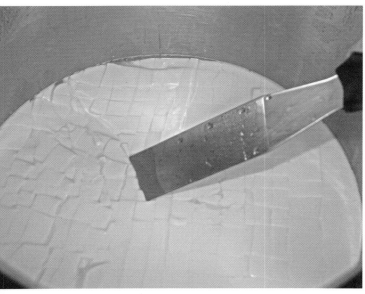

Curd is cut first into vertical columns, then at an angle as close to horizontal as possible.

curds.) Cutting exposes a lot of surface area, which allows the curds to quickly lose whey. Different types of cheeses have different goal curd sizes. Don't worry if your curds are not perfect cubes — no one's are — but do try to cut them as uniformly as possible. The first cuts create vertical columns (these are the easy ones). Next, the curds are cut horizontally; it is easier to make the horizontal cuts in a wide shallow pot than in a tall skinny one, so keep this in mind when choosing a vessel. After the cuts are made, most recipes call for "resting" or "healing" the curds for about 5 minutes. During this time, the curds will lose some whey from their surfaces. In doing so, they become a little less fragile, so that they don't break apart as easily when you start to stir in the next step.

Heat and Stir Curd

Most recipes produced by this method include a step in which the curds are heated (or "cooked") and stirred. (The exception in this chapter is feta) Just how hot and how much stirring is involved varies quite a bit. Whatever the instructions say, the stirring must be as gentle as possible to keep the curds from being shattered into pieces that are too small. In some cases, this may even mean gently shaking the pot for a while instead of using a spoon or ladle. After the curds have been moved around a little, they will shrink and firm up a bit so that you can stir them more easily.

If the recipe involves heating the curds, it is very important to do so as slowly as possible — especially in the beginning — and no faster than the recipe calls for. If you heat them too quickly, only the outside of the curd will dry and firm, leaving a mushy interior with whey trapped inside. Trapped whey can lead to brittle sour spots in the cheese. The goal of the heating and stirring step is to get the curds to the right texture for draining and pressing. For some cheeses, the goal texture is a tiny, very dry curd; for others, it's a larger, more tender curd.

The heating and stirring step is a test of patience and observation. It is tough to accomplish well if there are a lot of distractions or you attempt to multitask. (When I make cheese in our home kitchen, as opposed to our commercial creamery, I find it harder to stay on task for the entire process.)

Drain and Press

Once the texture of the curd is just right, the next steps involve removing the curd from the whey by draining the pot, and then removing the whey from the curd by pressing it. Some recipes call for pouring the curds and whey through a strainer or directly into the cheese forms, while others have you gather the curds into a ball while they are still submerged in the whey.

Once the curds have been removed from the whey, they are placed in a form. Almost all cheeses need to be drained and/or pressed in a cheesecloth-lined form. (There are a couple of exceptions, such as cheeses with large tender curds that won't have any weight applied to them, like feta.) You must pick a combination of form and cloth that allow the curd to drain as quickly as possible, but without letting any curd escape. If the form has a very open pattern of holes and you apply too much weight, curd might mush out through the holes. On the other hand, if the form doesn't have enough holes, the whey might not drain off of the cheese as quickly as you want, leaving whey trapped in the curd and an uneven pattern on the outside of the cheese.

During heating and stirring, the curds will shrink. (The whitish whey seen in this photo is typical in goat's milk cheesemaking.)

TIPS FOR STIRRING

1. Stir or agitate the curds as gently as possible; if they start shattering, you are stirring too roughly.

2. If any curds are too large, you can cut them into smaller pieces during the stirring step.

3. Once the curds move easily and don't break, stir only as gently as needed to keep them moving; if you stir too rapidly, they will become tough.

4. Pay close attention to how rapidly the curds are heated; heating more slowly in the beginning is always better than too fast.

TIPS FOR PRESSING

1. Choose a form and cloth that allow the curd to release a lot of whey, but don't allow the curd to pass through when pressed.
2. If the curd is getting stuck in the cheesecloth, the cloth has a weave that is too open or you are using too much weight.
3. Observe the cheese when it is flipped: The outside should be smooth and closed by the last flip. If it closes too early, you are using too much weight too soon. If it isn't closed by the end more weight is needed.
4. You only need a mechanical press for cheeses where the curd is salted before pressing, such as cheddar, or cheeses where the curd is very tiny and dry, such as Parmesan. Most cheeses can be pressed with other types of weights such as water jugs or barbells.

Weight is added to help remove the whey and to form the curds into a nice smooth wheel. Cheeses that have an open texture, such as feta, are not pressed, while those with a very tight, closed texture have a lot of weight applied. During the pressing phase, the cheese is unwrapped, flipped over, rewrapped, and pressed about 3 times. It is during these flips that you will decide if you are using enough pressure (see sidebar left).

You should think of the pressing phase as another ripening step. During pressing, not only will the cheese form into a wheel, but the bacteria will continue to grow and make acid (the exception is when curds are salted before pressing such as in cheddarmaking). For this reason, the temperature of the room during pressing is important. Some recipes call for the temperature to drop by the end of pressing, but usually room temperature, 68–72°F (20–22°C), is ideal. It is essential that the right amount of acid be produced, so that the cheese will be safe for aging and have a balanced flavor. If too much acid develops, the curd will be sour and brittle (the extra acid damages the invisible structure of the cheese curds causing them to break apart). The home cheesemaker may not have the ability to measure this acid production with a pH meter (and pH strips won't work for checking solid cheese curd), but over time you can train your taste buds to detect the perfect sourness.

Salt

Once you have finished draining and pressing the cheese, it is important to both cool and salt it. By cooling the cheese, you quickly slow and then stop the growth of the bacteria, which will help prevent the cheese from getting too sour and possibly become brittle during aging. As you learned in chapter 2, salt will help stop the bacteria from growing too, but if the cheese is thick, the salt won't make it all of the way to the center of the wheel for several days.

If you are dry salting, rub the first coat on all sides of the cheese, rewrap it in the cheesecloth, and replace it in the form. Set the cheese in a cool area, ideally about 50–55°F (10–12°C). By rewrapping the cheese you will help keep the salt close to the wheel and also prevent the cheese from changing shape before it cools and firms. The second coat of salt should be applied as the specific lesson indicates.

Store and Use

All of the cheeses in this chapter can be used immediately after they are finished; you don't really even need to chill them. Some will benefit from a few days of resting in the refrigerator, though, as the salt and flavors will have a chance to comingle and smooth out. Many will last weeks in the fridge as long as they are tightly wrapped and protected from contaminating yeasts and molds. A little surface mold can simply be cut away and the rest of the cheese used.

WHAT TO DO WITH THE WHEY FROM RENNET-COAGULATED FRESH CHEESES

The whey that is produced during the lessons in this chapter (with the exception of quick mozzarella [lesson 12]) — and all similar recipes — contains many nutrients and some starter culture bacteria. The nutrients consist of a lot of whey protein, calcium and some milk sugar. Because the fresh whey from these cheeses isn't very acidic (in fact, it is called sweet whey), it can be used for a variety of things, including making whey ricotta (see bonus recipe in chapter 8). In the kitchen, fresh sweet whey is great in soups, when making bread, and can even be used as a beverage (either plain or flavored) or to boost start the lacto-fermentation of vegetables.

Dry salting a cheese.

It can also be fed to chickens, pigs, and even calves. Because of the nutrients in the whey, it shouldn't be poured down drains in large volumes, but the home cheesemaker doesn't need to worry about that too much.

LESSON 12: QUICK MOZZARELLA

Quick mozzarella is truly a miracle process, but one that may not work perfectly every time if the milk you use varies a lot. It is one of those recipes that initially seems foolproof when demonstrated to beginning cheesemakers, but in fact is not. Traditional mozzarella takes all day to make, uses starter culture bacteria for flavor and acid, and can be aged. Quick mozzarella, on the other hand, has added acid, more rennet, and can often be made in under an hour. The longer method definitely produces a more complex cheese with better texture, but the tradeoff is about five hours of your day! I recommend using store-bought whole cow's milk the first few times you make the quick version. Because this type of milk is mass-produced, it is less variable and, therefore, less likely to misbehave. After you get a good feel for the process, give it a try on whatever other milk you prefer.

Mozzarella is in a category of cheese called *pasta filata*, which is Italian for stretched or kneaded dough. Most of the cheeses in this family, such as *Kashkaval, caciocavallo,* and *provolone,* are from Mediterranean countries. Latin American countries also produce traditional cheeses in this group, including *Oaxaca,* which is formed into a beautiful skein that you unroll as you use the cheese. Stretched-curd cheeses rely upon a precise balance of minerals in the curd, acid content, and temperature. If any of these things is not just right, the stretch will be less than ideal or nonexistent. But don't be intimidated — I have yet to have the following recipe not work!

What You'll Need

Milk: 1 gal. (4 L) cold whole to partly skimmed milk

Acid: 1½ tsp. (7.5 g) citric acid diluted in ⅛ cup (30 ml) cool water

Rennet: ⅛ tsp. (0.75 ml) double-strength vegetarian rennet diluted in ⅛ cup (30 ml) cool, non-chlorinated water

Salt: ½ tsp. (2.5 g) pure salt

Equipment: Two pots, thermometer, ladle, colander, heavy gloves, large bowl

Process in a Nutshell

Time: 60–90 min.

Steps: Add acid, heat milk, add rennet, cut curd, heat and stir curd, drain, prepare whey, stretch curd, chill, store and use.

Step by Step

Add Acid: Pour the cold milk into one of the pots. Add the diluted acid and, using the ladle, stir together well.

Heat Milk: Place the pot over medium heat or in a water bath on the stovetop. Heat the milk until it reaches 88°F–90°F (31°C–32°C). Turn off the heat.

Rennet and Coagulate: Stir the milk using an up-and-down motion with the ladle. Stop stirring briefly and pour the diluted rennet over the top of the ladle. Begin stirring up and down again for 10 seconds. Hold the ladle to the top of the milk in several spots to help still the milk. Let the curd set until a clean break is achieved, about 5 minutes.

Cut Curd: Cut the curd into ¼-inch to ½-inch (6 to 12 mm) cubes.

Heat and Stir Curd: Heat the curds very gradually, stirring gently, to 105°F (41°C) over 5–10 minutes.

Drain: Remove the pot from the heat. Position the colander over the second pot. Pour or ladle the curds into the colander and let the whey drain while you do the next step.

Prepare Whey: Add the salt to the pot with the whey. Place the pot over medium-high heat and heat the whey until the temperature reaches 150°F (66°C). Tear off a small piece of the reserved drained curd and place it in the ladle. Immerse the curd in the hot whey for about 15 seconds and pull it out again. Gently squeeze and pull the curd to see if it will stretch. If not, heat the whey another 10°F (6°C) and test the curd again.

Cut and Stretch Curd: Maintain the whey at the temperature at which your test piece stretched. Cut the curd mass into quarters. Working with one piece of curd at a time, place the curd in the bowl of the ladle and immerse it in the hot whey until it is pliable, 30–60 seconds. Pull the curd out and work it gently as shown in the photo below; be very gentle and try to not over-work it. Reheat the curd as needed to maintain a pliable texture. Repeat the process about three times until the curd feels smooth and looks shiny; reserve the whey.

Chill: Fill the bowl with cold water. Place the formed balls in the water to chill and set the shape.

Store and Use: Use the mozzarella within a few hours, or chill some of the salted whey and store the mozzarella in it and refrigerate for up to 7 days. If you want to use the mozzarella for

Mozzarella stretches perfectly when the acid level and temperature are just right.

pizza, wrap the balls in plastic and refrigerate for up to 1 week; it will melt beautifully after the first 2 days.

Troubleshooting

Curd is grainy, crumbly, won't stretch: Too much acid, try using about ¼ tsp. (1gm) less next time. Be sure to measure the citric acid very carefully.

Curd is firm, breaks when stretched: Not enough citric acid, try using about ¼ tsp. (1gm) more next time. Again, be sure to measure the citric acid very carefully.

Curd stretched well, but end result is rubbery and bouncy: Curd is overstretched, overworked, or overheated. It is easy to squeeze out the butterfat during stretching. If the temperature of the whey is too hot, it can also melt the fat out of the curd. Keep practicing and be very gentle.

Recap

This cheese is a demonstration not only of how curd behaves, but also of how you can easily (and often accidentally) change its properties. The chemistry of making mozzarella is pretty fascinating: you are using acid and heat to manipulate the minerals and the way the curd structure moves — and in quite a different fashion than in the high-heat added-acid cheeses in chapter 4. If you ever move on to making traditional mozzarella (and I hope you will), you will be doing the same manipulation, but by using the starter bacteria to make just the right amount of acid — this is the time-consuming part. If you had fun making mozzarella, you will probably love the bonus recipe below for little stuffed pillows of stretched curd cheese: *burrata.*

BONUS RECIPE: BURRATA

This recipe is just for fun — and deliciousness! It combines the above recipe for making mozzarella with a recipe for making ricotta using whey and milk. Making the dumplings turn out just the way you want may take a bit of practice, but the results are worth it. And no matter how they turn out, you can still eat them!

Burrata, or *burratina*, is a rather new cheese that was created in the early 1900s as a way to use up bits of curd left over from forming mozzarella. Its name comes from *burra*, the Italian word for butter, and refers to the buttery texture of the filling. The recipe I have provided here includes a bit of butter in the filling, but you can have fun with it and fill burrata with some fairly creative combinations including ricotta and blue cheese, seasoned ricotta, and bits of mozzarella curd. On a 2015 trip to Italy, we enjoyed *burratina affumicata*, a tender, moist burrata that had been smoked in a tiny basket and served on a bed of fresh arugula.

What You'll Need

Same as the recipe above for quick mozzarella, plus:

Milk: 1 qt. (1 L) whole milk

Burrata stuffed with fresh ricotta and butter, dressed with olive oil and fresh thyme.

Acid: 1 tsp. (5 g) citric acid diluted in ⅛ cup (30 ml) cold water

Butter: 1 tbsp. (14 g) unsalted or salted butter

Seasoning: Salt and pepper to taste

Salt: 1 tsp. (5 g) pure salt

Equipment: Fine-mesh sieve, spatula, 2 small bowls, ladle, plate, serving spoon, ladle, heavy gloves

Process in a Nutshell

Time: 2 hr. active

Step by Step

Follow the recipe for quick mozzarella above to just before you stretch the curd, and then continue with the following steps:

Heat Whey: Pour the milk into the pot with the whey, and place the pot over medium-high heat. Heat the mixture, stirring gently, until the temperature reaches 175°F (79°C) and it coagulates into curds.

Add Acid: If the liquid is still white and milky, stir in the diluted citric acid solution. Remove the pot from the heat and let set for 5 minutes.

Drain Curd: Using the small sieve, skim the curds from the top of the whey and let drain over the pot for about 3 minutes.

Finish Filling: Using the spatula, scrape the ricotta into the bowl. Stir in the butter and salt and pepper to taste. Set aside.

For the dumplings:

Heat Whey: Stir the pure salt into the whey. Check that the temperature of the whey is still 175°F (79°C).

After stretching and pressing the curd into a disc, the ricotta mixture is added to the center.

Cut and Stretch Curd: Cut the curd mass into 10–12 even pieces. Working with one piece of curd at a time, place the curd in the ladle and immerse it the hot whey until it is pliable, 10–20 seconds. Place it on the plate and gently work it by folding it in toward the center in a circular pattern and pressing softly down; reheat the curd as needed to maintain a pliable texture. Repeat the process about two times just until the curd feels smooth and looks shiny. Use your fingers to shape it into a flat patty about 3 inches by 3 inches (7 cm by 7 cm).

Fill and Form Dumplings: Working with one patty at a time, spoon a small amount of the ricotta filling into the center. To form the packet, bring two opposite sides of the curd patty together, then the other two, making a small purse. Press the top of the gathered edges gently over and lay it, gathered-side down, onto the ladle. Carefully immerse the dumpling in the hot whey until the edges are sealed, 5–8 seconds.

Chill: Serve the burrata immediately, or fill the second bowl with cold water and place the dumplings in the water just long enough to firm them up, about 10 minutes.

Store and Use: Use the burrata within a day for the best texture. Serve alone or drizzled with a high-quality aged balsamic vinegar, chopped fresh basil, and garden-fresh tomatoes, or use in any recipe calling for burrata.

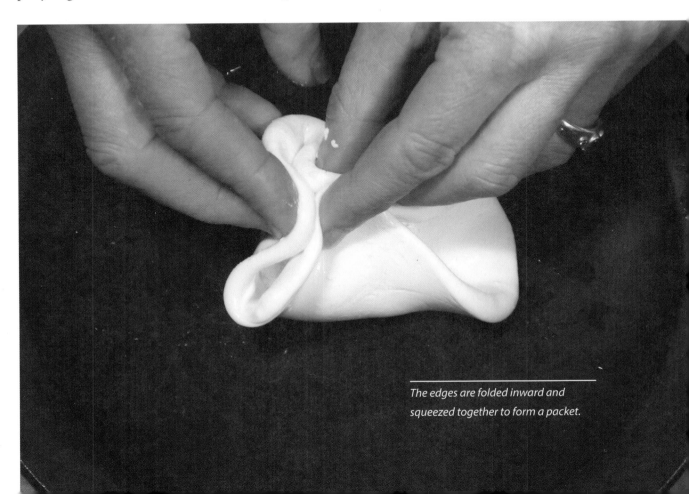

The edges are folded inward and squeezed together to form a packet.

LESSON 13: FETA

I often refer to feta as the gateway cheese, not because it will transform someone who doesn't like cheese into a cheese lover, but because it is the perfect first cheese for those wanting to learn how to make more complicated cheeses such as those in the next chapter. Feta can also easily be aged, even at home with no special equipment. It is the ideal cheese to make now and enjoy later.

The name "feta" is most correctly applied to this cheese when it is made in Greece and uses mostly sheep's milk and a bit of goat's milk. But many other countries have made virtually identical products by other names. Whatever you call it, this cheese is salty, tangy, and may be crumbly and dry or soft and creamy depending on the techniques used during cheesemaking. Feta and its Mediterranean cousins such as *Telemes*, a cow's milk version, are salty because they are preserved in brine. Salt has long been a way of preserving food, and in seaside countries, it lent its talent to preserving cheese. Even when stored in heavy salt, feta continues to age, developing flavor and changing in texture. I'm going to explain how to salt it for use now and later, and also how to age it in an oil marinade.

What You'll Need

Milk: 1 gal. (4 L) whole to partly skimmed milk

Culture: ⅛ tsp. (0.2 g) Flora Danica

Calcium Chloride (optional): ⅛ tsp. (0.7 ml) calcium chloride diluted in ⅛ cup (30 ml) cool water

Rennet: 1/16 tsp (0.35 ml) double-strength vegetarian rennet diluted in ⅛ cup (30 ml) cool, non-chlorinated water

Salt: 2 tbsp. (30 g) pure salt

Equipment: Pot, thermometer, ladle, cheesecloth, colander, tub with a lid

Process in a Nutshell

Time: 2½ hr. active, 12 hr. inactive

Steps: Heat milk, add culture, ripen, add calcium chloride (if using), add rennet, ripen and coagulate, cut curd, heat and stir curd, drain, salt, store and use

Step by Step

Heat Milk: Pour the milk into the pot, and set the pot into a warm-water bath. Heat the milk until the temperature reaches 88–90°F (31–32°C).

Add Culture: Sprinkle the culture on top of milk and let it set for 3–5 minutes. Stir gently for 2–5 minutes.

Ripen: Maintain the temperature of the milk at 88°F–90°F (31°C–32°C), stirring occasionally, and let ripen for 1 hour.

Add Calcium Chloride (optional): Stir in the diluted calcium chloride, if using, and let set for 5 minutes.

Add Rennet: Stir the milk using an up-and-down motion with the ladle. Stop stirring briefly and pour the diluted rennet over the top of the

Feta can be marinated and aged in oil with herbs, spices, and other ingredients such as sun dried tomatoes.

ladle. Begin stirring again for 1 minute. Hold the ladle to the top of the milk in several spots to help still the milk.

Coagulate: Maintain the temperature of the milk at 88–90°F (31–32°C), and let the curd set until a clean break is achieved, about 45 minutes.

Cut Curd: Cut the curd mass into ¾-inch to 1-inch (2 cm to 3 cm) cubes, and let rest for 10–15 minutes.

Heat and Stir Curd: Maintain the temperature of the curds at 88–90°F (31–32°C) and stir gently for 20 minutes; the curds will be very tender and soft. Let the curds rest for 5 minutes.

Drain: Position the colander over another pot and line it with the cheesecloth. Carefully ladle most of the curds from the pot into the lined colander. Gently pour the rest of the curds and whey into the colander. Tie the corners of the cheesecloth together. Tie the bundle to the handle of the ladle and set across the top of the pot. Allow the curds to drain at room temperature, 68–72°F (20–22°C) for 12 hours. The bundle should not touch the whey; drain the whey if too much collects at the bottom. If needed, you can tighten the bag a bit, but don't squeeze the curds.

Salt: Unwrap the feta and cut it into 1-inch-thick (3 cm thick) slabs. Sprinkle salt on all sides of these slabs and place in the tub and cover or a zipper-lock bag. Let set at room temperature, turning occasionally to coat with the salt and whey, for 8 hours.

Store and Use: Use the fresh feta right away, or tightly cover and refrigerate.

Variations

Aging or storing in brine: Follow the steps above and reserve the salty whey from the salting step. Pack the slabs as tightly as possible in a tub or jar, filling the spaces with bits of the cheese that might break off or not fit otherwise, and pour the reserved brine over the top. Add 1 teaspoon (5 g) of pure salt and let set at room temperature, 68°F–72°F (20°C–22°C), for 8 hours. The cheese should create its own brine. If there is still airspace in the tub but the brine covers the cheese, cover the cheese and brine with a piece of plastic wrap, and then put the lid on the tub. Let age for several weeks to months. Check the cheese occasionally for flavor and texture.

Aging or storing in oil: Follow the steps above for fresh feta, but let the cheese mellow for 3 days in the refrigerator. During this time, drain the brine from it daily. Cut the slabs into bite-sized cubes and place in a glass jar. Cover the cubes with olive oil or a mixture of olive oil and another oil, less likely to solidify such as rice bran oil, and screw the lid on the jar. Don't use olive oil that is too high-quality, or the flavor will overwhelm the cheese. You can add herbs to the oil, if desired. Age the marinated cheese in the back of the refrigerator for up to one year.

Troubleshooting

Curd of the finished cheese is sponge-like with hundreds of small, oval shaped holes (or eyes): This is called "early blowing" and is a sign of contamination by coliform bacteria. Coliforms are from the environment and can be harmless, but may also include some extremely dangerous disease-causing germs. They can contaminate raw milk or be introduced into pasteurized milk after it is heat treated. Throw the batch out and improve your equipment sanitation. If you are using raw milk, choose a different source (see chapter 2).

Too salty: Feta is supposed to be salty, so this is not necessarily a legitimate problem. But if you prefer yours less salty, add less salt and don't age it. For feta that is aged in brine, you can soak it briefly in water, or even milk, to rinse away much of the salt before using.

Not tangy enough: The room was probably not warm enough during draining. Try not letting the temperature drop below 72°F (22°C) if possible, or hanging the curds for an hour or so longer to let more acid develop.

Too soft: Some milk types will naturally result in a softer feta, but cutting the curds too small or squeezing them too much during draining can also lead to a softer cheese. The curds need to retain enough whey during draining to help develop acid. (It's the acid that helps make the cheese more crumbly.) Also make sure that the room is the right temperature during draining so that the bacteria can make enough acid. (If the curds are soft because not enough acid is made, they also probably won't taste tangy enough.)

Got soft during aging in brine: This means that there was not enough calcium in the milk and, therefore, in the whey brine. Remove the soft cheese from the tub and make a new brine of 1 quart (500 ml) water, 6 tbsp. (90 g) pure salt, ½ tsp. (2.5 ml) white or cider vinegar, and 1 tsp. (5 ml) calcium chloride. Next time add calcium chloride to the natural brine in the tub before aging.

Recap

Feta is such a versatile cheese. You can use it on and in just about anything, often foregoing added salt. The fact that it is so easy to age also makes it a great cheese to have on hand. You can add flavors such as herbs and spices to the curd just before draining or to an oil marinade.

Feta can be aged in a salt water brine in the fridge for many months while it develops flavor and a creamy texture. These square slabs where first made by draining the curd in a homemade form that was of the same shape. The plastic film on top helps prevent mold from developing on the cheese during aging.

LESSON 14: FARMHOUSE CHEESE

Farmhouse, farmstead, farmer's, cottage, landholder — all of these terms have been applied to simple cheeses made to be eaten young or slightly aged. Usually made from raw milk and lightly cooked and lightly pressed, they are simple, pleasant, and versatile. Because the curd is stirred and heated a bit, and much of the whey is removed by pressing, these cheeses have a longer shelf life than the paneer in chapter 4. This recipe can also be used for making an aged version, but try it first as a fresh cheese. It is a great one to boost your confidence and get you ready for the next step on your journey.

What You'll Need

Milk: 2 gal. (8 L) whole milk

Culture: ¼ tsp. (0.4 g) Flora Danica

Calcium Chloride (optional): ¼ tsp. (1.25 ml) calcium chloride diluted in ¼ cup (60 ml) cool water

Rennet: ⅛ tsp. (0.7 ml) double-strength vegetarian rennet diluted just before use in ¼ cup (60 ml) cool, non-chlorinated water

Salt: 2 tbsp. (30 g) pure salt

Equipment: Pot, thermometer, ladle, cheesecloth, tray, form, water jug or other weight for pressing, tub with lid

Process in a Nutshell

Time: 3 hr. active, 4–6 hr. plus 3 days inactive

Steps: Heat milk, add culture, ripen, add rennet, ripen and coagulate, cut curd, heat and stir curd, partial drain, drain and press, salt, store and use

Step by Step

Heat Milk: Pour the milk into the pot, and place the pot over another pot of water on the stovetop. Heat the milk until the temperature reaches 88–90°F (31–32°C).

Add Culture: Sprinkle the culture on top of milk and let it set for 3–5 minutes. Stir gently for 2–5 minutes.

Ripen: Maintain the temperature of the milk at 88–90°F (31–32°C), stirring occasionally, and let ripen for 30 minutes.

Add Calcium Chloride (optional): Stir in the diluted calcium chloride, if using, and let set for 5 minutes.

Add Rennet: Stir the milk using an up-and-down motion with the ladle. Stop stirring briefly and pour the diluted rennet over the top of the ladle. Begin stirring again for 1 minute. Hold the ladle to the top of the milk in several spots to help still the milk.

Coagulate: Maintain the temperature of the milk at 88–90°F (31–32°C), and let the curd set until a clean break is achieved, about 45 minutes.

Cut Curd: Cut the curd mass into ⅜-inch (1 cm) cubes, and let rest for 5 minutes.

Heat and Stir Curd: Heat the curds very gradually, stirring gently, to 100°F (38°C) over 30 minutes; increase the temperature a bit more slowly in the beginning, especially during the first 15 minutes. If needed, cut any large curds into smaller pieces during stirring.

Maintain the temperature of the curds at 100°F (38°C) for 20 minutes, stirring constantly and gently until the curds are uniform in size and feel tender but springy, similar to the texture of a hard-boiled egg white, about 15 minutes. Remove the pot from the heat and let the curds set for 5 minutes.

Partial Drain: Scoop out the whey to the level of the curds; reserve some of the whey. Using your hands, work the curds gently into a solid mass about the size of the form that you are using.

Drain and Press: Place the form on a tray or a drainboard. Line the form with the cheesecloth and dampen it with a bit of whey. Using your hands, lift the curd mass out of the pot and press it gently into the form. When it evenly fills the

The curd (here flavored with red pepper) is scooped into a cheesecloth lined form and then pressed lightly for about 6 hours.

form, fold the excess cloth over the curd, set the follower on top, and press down gently. Add about 1 pound (0.5 kg) of weight. Press for 15 minutes at room temperature, 68–72°F (20–22°C).

Remove the weight and the follower. Then remove the wrapped cheese from the form, unwrap it, and flip it over. Rearrange the cheesecloth in the form, and then replace the cheese, pressing the cloth into the form along with it; the cheese should still look a bit wrinkled and the rind not yet smooth. Continue to press with only 1 pound (0.5 kg) of weight for 30 minutes more.

Repeat the steps above, flipping the cheese and rearranging it in the form; this time the rind should be smoother, but still not evenly closed. Add another 1 pound (0.5 kg) of weight for a total of 2 pounds (1 kg) and continue to press for 60 minutes more.

Repeat the steps again; now the rind should be very even, perhaps with a few small openings. If not, you may add up to 2 pounds more weight. Continue to press for 4 hours more.

Remove the cheese from the form, cut off a tiny piece, and taste it. It should have a very mild tang and taste milky with a hint of buttermilk. If it isn't slightly tangy, press it for 1 hour more and taste it again.

Salt: When you have achieved the desired tang, take the cheese from the form, unwrap, and rub the cheese all over with 1 tbsp. (15 g) of the salt. Replace the cheese in the form, without the cheesecloth, and let it set for 30 minutes. Remove the cheese and rub it with the remaining 1 tbsp. (15 g) of salt.

Place the cheese in the tub, cover, and let it set in the refrigerator for 8–12 hours. After

setting, there may be a bit of salty whey at the bottom of the tub; if so, rub the whey all over the cheese and flip it over. Repeat this process 2–3 times daily for the next 3 days. During this time, the cheese will change in texture and flavor as the salt moves through the wheel and the cheese mellows.

Store and Use: Pat the cheese dry with paper towels and wrap tightly in plastic wrap or a plastic bag. Use or store in the refrigerator for up to 4 weeks. It will last longer and even age if there is very little air in the container and exposure to molds in the air outside of the fridge is limited. If a little mold develops on the outside, either cut it off before eating, or rub it with a bit of vinegar.

Troubleshooting

Curd of the finished cheese is sponge-like with hundreds of small, oval shaped holes (or eyes): This is called "early blowing" and is a sign of contamination by coliform bacteria. Coliforms are from the environment and can be harmless but may also include some extremely dangerous disease-causing microbes. They can contaminate raw milk or be introduced into pasteurized milk after it is heat treated. Throw the batch out and consider choosing a different source if you are buying raw milk (see chapter 2); also improve your sanitation and preparation of equipment.

Wrinkles or openings in rind after pressing: You probably did not apply enough pressure and/or the room got too cool. You can usually fix this problem at the end of pressing by heating a pot of water to about 160°F (71°C) and then immersing the wheel into the hot water for 1–2 minutes. Quickly replace the cheese in the form with double the original weight and press for 10 minutes. This should smooth out the surface.

Cheese tastes bland: Use ⅛ tsp. (0.2 g) more culture the next time or extend the ripening phase by about 15 minutes. Also make sure the room isn't too cool during pressing. When young, this isn't a super complex cheese by any means, but it shouldn't be super boring either.

Cheese tastes sour: Next time try either using ⅛ tsp. (0.2 g) less culture or shortening the pressing time by about 15 minutes. Also be sure that the room isn't too warm during pressing and salting.

Recap

Let's consider the differences between this recipe and feta. You can certainly see and taste that the farmhouse cheese is not as salty, crumbly, and tangy as feta. You will notice some close similarities in the first few steps of the cheese-making process, but then see how they diverge during the stirring phase. The feta curd wasn't cooked and therefore retained more moisture. That moisture helped create the crumbly texture and tartness that are the hallmarks of feta. When curd is stirred and heated for longer, it loses more moisture earlier. This has a profound effect on the final texture of the cheese. Let's move on to the next level: cheeses for aging.

After dry salting the farmhouse cheese, this one with added hot pepper flakes and an infusion (see page 26, 27 for more), is ready to eat.

NOTES

8: RENNET-COAGULATED AGED CHEESES

ONLY GOOD CHEESE can become great aged cheese, but even a good cheese won't survive poor aging techniques. As I mentioned earlier, I one day hope to devote an entire book simply to the subject of *affinage,* the art of aging cheeses. But for this book, I have limited the discussion to some methods that should ensure success at home without having to buy fancy equipment or deal with the growth of molds, the problems of humidity control, and the possible invasion of cheese mites.

The vast majority of cheeses consumed in the world are aged, to one degree or another, and most of these are semi-hard to hard. The classic cheeses that we will be covering in this chapter belong to this group. When attempting these cheeses, don't be surprised when your homemade cheese does not mirror the industrial version! That's a good thing, but it can take some getting used to.

The hardest thing for most new cheesemakers to do is to wait. It can be especially hard to wait long enough for a cheese to age. Don't feel too badly if you fall victim to cutting into a wheel before time. Fortunately, when using vacuum sealing to protect cheese during aging, you can simply seal the bag back up and let the cut cheese age longer.

STEPS FOR MAKING RENNET-COAGULATED AGED CHEESES

Most of the steps in this method are the same as in the last chapter. The big differences come during the salting and aging steps, which I will cover here. (Please review the tips and steps of the last chapter if you need to.) Cheeses in this category will usually yield about 0.85–1.1 pounds per gallon of milk (0.4–0.5 kg per 4 L), depending on how they are pressed, salted, and aged.

Salting

Some cheeses are ready to salt before they are pressed, such as cheddar types. In that case, the salt is added to the curds in a minimum of two additions, sprinkling it on, letting it sit (called *mellowing*), and stirring.

Floating and soaking a pressed cheese in a saltwater solution, or brine, is the best way to salt many types of cheeses. When brining, the cheese is floated in a saltwater solution for a period of hours. The top is sprinkled with a handful of dry salt (my preferred method), or the cheese is turned halfway through its time in the brine bath. Pour the brine into a container large enough to hold the cheese, leaving room around all sides for the brine to circulate. After the cheese is finished soaking, pour the brine and any extra salt from the top of the cheese through a cloth lined sieve and back into the jugs and refrigerate.

Aging

Cheeses can age under a great variety of conditions and still turn out great. (I've even seen

HOW TO MAKE A HEAVY BRINE

Combine 1 gallon (4 L) non-chlorinated water at room temperature, 1 tablespoon (15 ml) calcium chloride, and 2 teaspoons white or cider vinegar. Add 2.5 pounds (1 kg) of salt and stir until mostly dissolved. If it dissolves completely, add more salt until the solution will not hold any more salt. This makes what is called a fully saturated brine. Basically, as long as you can see some salt at the bottom of the solution, there is enough salt in the brine. The brine can be reused for many batches of cheese over many months. It should be stored in the refrigerator between use and filtered through a cheesecloth between batches, especially if any tiny curd particles are left by cheeses that have been floating in the brine. Let the brine come to about 50–55°F (10 to 12°C) before use and keep it at that temperature while cheese is being brined.

Brine can be made using the whey from cheesemaking. Add the same amount of salt as indicated and omit the vinegar and calcium chloride. Whey brines are more subject to getting too sour, unless they are heavily salted and kept cold, so if you try this method, test the brine for sourness now and then.

THE MISCONCEPTION OF THE AIR-DRYING PHASE

I can't tell you how many cheesemakers I have met — licensed commercial cheesemakers — who still subject their beautiful wheels of cheese to an air-drying period. This step is a common one in some beginning cheesemaking books, but is not necessary when the cheese is to be aged naturally. Even if you plan on waxing or vacuum sealing the cheese, you do not want to let the cheese sit out in a dry, comfortably warm room. As you just learned, the cooling process is very important to stopping bacterial growth inside the cheese. If the cheese is left out in a warm dry room, not only do you risk more bacterial growth, but also you are very likely to dry the surface of the cheese so much that it will crack immediately or later. The cheese surface can be adequately dried in a cool room with the humidity low enough to allow surface drying but not dehydration of the cheese itself. If the humidity is too low, the cheese will dry out too much at the surface, will likely have a really thick rind, and may even crack.

Accomplished home cheesemaker Elizabeth Boutin, Washington, checks a variety of cheeses being aged using vacuum sealing, waxing, and natural rinds in a large wine refrigerator/cooler.

it successfully done on open shelves in a jungle environment.) The finest artisan cheeses, though, are aged under very strict, difficult-to-maintain conditions. I devote an entire chapter to it in *Mastering Artisan Cheesemaking*, but the subject deserves an entire book. For our lessons though, I want to make things as simple — and as likely to succeed — as possible, so we will be aging cheeses in a regular refrigerator using tubs and vacuum sealing. A natural rind can also be created by aging in a tub in a wine cooler fridge. Waxing is also an option, but I find it much less successful than vacuum sealing, in addition to being messy and awkward.

Vacuum Bag Aging

This is the easiest method and requires almost zero follow-through during the aging process. The cheeses will age more slowly and without quite the complexity as when aged traditionally with a natural rind. There is a definite trade-off, but your life circumstances will make one or the other more likely to succeed, and that is the ultimate goal of this book.

To prepare a cheese for vacuum sealing, its moisture content must first stabilize; otherwise liquid will leak from the cheese and pool in the bag. Some of the cheeses we will make in chapter 8 are dry enough, thanks to the curd being salted before the cheese is pressed, to vacuum seal immediately. But some cheeses will need to sit for several days while their moisture content stabilizes. For this process, I recommend using a lidded tub large enough to comfortably hold the cheese without touching it. Set the cheese on a mat on top of a rack at the bottom of the tub. The tub should be set in a cool place, between 40°F (4.4°C) and 50°F (10°C). Flip the cheese daily and use a clean towel or paper towel to wipe away any humidity that collects on the lid or sides. If there is a lot of moisture on the lid, place a second mat over the cheese and a towel over that; change the towel under the mat if it grows moist. After about 10 days, the cheese should be ready to vacuum seal.

Once sealed, place the cheese in your aging space, whether the refrigerator or a wine cooler (see chapter 3), and check it daily. Flipping the cheese every few days is also a good idea, but not as critical as it is for a cheese that is aged without sealing. If any moisture does collect, open the bag, dry the cheese with a towel, and reseal.

Natural Rind Aging

If you have more time and don't mind doing a little cheese maintenance, then aging a cheese without sealing it can be a wonderful way to create a distinctive, flavorful product. You have to prepare yourself, though, for accepting a certain amount of mold and blemishes. Naturally rinded cheeses can look a bit gnarly at times, but there is nothing to fear! Time and a bit of effort will transform them into delicious masterpieces.

To prepare a cheese for aging naturally, ensure that after pressing the cheese the rind is fully closed — without cracks or holes. If there are any cracks, the molds that will otherwise be harmless, will grow inside the cheese and damage the flavor. If there are lines from the cheesecloth, that's okay, except that they will have more mold growing in them than if the cheese were smooth. After the cheese has been salted or brined, it is ready to go directly into aging. Place a cheese mat on a rack in the bottom of a tub that is larger than the wheel of cheese. You can age several cheeses at a time in the same tub. Place the cheese on the mat and place the lid on the tub. Place the tub in a refrigerator or preferably a wine or beverage cooler. These types of appliances can be set to 50–55°F (10–12°C), which is the ideal temperature for aging cheese.

Open the tub and turn the cheese daily for the first 4 weeks, then twice a week until it is done. If there is excess moisture in the tub, dry it with a cloth. But if the tub is too dry and the surface of the cheese is becoming overly dry — watch for cracks and hardening — then place a damp paper towel (or several) in the box with the cheese. When molds develop, and they will, take a clean, dry cloth (such as a cheesecloth) or a soft bristle brush and gently pat, rub, or brush the surface of the cheese. The goal is not necessarily to eliminate all of the molds, but to slow their growth. Over time, the molds will contribute to creating a beautiful, rustic finish on the cheese.

Please note that since natural rind aging leads to some moisture loss and drying in the cheese, the size of the wheel must be large enough to allow for this. For that reason, I highly recommend that natural rind cheeses aged over 6 months be larger than the 2-gallon (8 L) batches that the recipes in this chapter indicate. I suggest doubling the recipes at the minimum, to allow for the natural shrinkage that will occur during natural rind aging.

Store and Use

Once the cheese has finished aging and the wheel is opened, it can be stored in the refrigerator and used as desired for an extended period of time, even months. If any surface mold develops, it can be scraped or cut off. It is important to protect the cheese from absorbing off flavors and over drying simply to preserve its flavor — and to honor all of the work you have put into making it!

Beginning cheesemaker Amanda Nunez gently patting down the molds on a wheel of aging cheese. Notice that the rind looks tender and not overly dry (the lines are from where the cheese was resting on a reed mat).

LESSON 15: GOUDA

No matter how you say it (*GOO-duh, HOW-duh,* or *GOW-duh*), this Dutch classic is well-known throughout the world and appears in many guises. Industrial red and black waxed grocery-store wheels; processed, artificial smoke–flavored slices; and huge, masterfully aged, crystalline artisan wheels are some of the cheeses that bear the name Gouda. While most of us are used to seeing waxed versions (and, I admit, they do look pretty), waxing is not a traditional step, but originally was done to help preserve the wheels during long overseas shipments before refrigeration was available. So don't feel that your Gouda is less authentic if you don't coat it with a thick layer of wax!

This recipe introduces a process step that is unique to some cheeses: washing the curd. *Washed-curd* cheeses are typically much more supple and mild, especially when young. They are pleasant and easy to slice and melt unless aged for a great deal of time. I adore washed-curd cheeses; they offer a lot of variety as they age and appeal to a broad spectrum of cheese eaters.

What You'll Need

Milk: 2 gal. (8 L) whole milk

Culture: ⅛ tsp. (0.2 g) MA 4000

Calcium Chloride (optional): ¼ tsp (1.25 ml) calcium chloride diluted in ⅛ cup (30 ml) cool water

Rennet: ⅛ tsp (0.75 ml) double-strength vegetarian rennet diluted just before use in ⅛ cup (30 ml) cool, non-chlorinated water

Salt: Heavy brine (see chapter 3 for recipe) and pure salt

Equipment: Pot, thermometer, ladle, measuring cup, cheesecloth, tray or drainboard, cheese form and weights or cheese press with form, tub with lid, mat, rack,1 gal. (4 L) vacuum-sealable bag and vacuum sealer

Process in a Nutshell

Time: 3 hr. active, 7 hr. inactive

Steps: Heat milk, add culture, ripen, add rennet, ripen and coagulate, cut curd, stir curd, wash, heat and stir curd, partial drain, drain and press, salt, age, store and use

Step by Step

Heat Milk: Pour the milk into the pot, and place the pot over another pot of water on the stovetop. Heat the milk until the temperature reaches 88–90°F (31–32°C).

Add Culture: Sprinkle the culture on top of milk and let set for 3–5 minutes. Using the ladle, stir gently for 2–5 minutes.

Ripen: Maintain the temperature of the milk at 88°F–90°F (31°C–32°C), stirring occasionally, and let ripen for 45 minutes.

Add Calcium Chloride (optional): Stir in the diluted calcium chloride, if using, and let set for 5 minutes.

Canadian cheesemaker Ian Treuer makes a large variety of cheeses, including this spice-rubbed, aged Gouda.

Photo by and courtesy of Ian Treuer

Add Rennet: Stir the milk using an up-and-down motion with the ladle. Stop stirring briefly and pour the diluted rennet over the top of the ladle. Begin stirring again for 1 minute. Hold the ladle to the top of the milk in several spots to help still the milk.

Coagulate: Maintain the temperature of the milk at 88–90°F (31–32°C), and let the curd set until a clean break is achieved, about 45 minutes.

Cut Curd: Cut the curd mass into ³⁄₈-inch (1 cm) cubes, and let rest at 88–90°F (31–32°C) for 5 minutes.

Stir Curd: Maintain the temperature of the curds at 88°F–90°F (31°C–32°C), stirring gently, for 15–20 minutes. If needed, cut any large curds into smaller pieces during stirring. Let the curds settle for 5 minutes; they will have shrunk some, but will still be quite soft.

Wash, Heat, and Stir Curd: Scoop out 2–2.5 qt. (2–2.5 L) of the whey. Stir the curds to break them apart. While stirring, add 150°F (66°C) hot water in 1 cup (250 ml) increments until the whey temperature is 101°F (38°C); this should take about 10 minutes. Continue stirring until the curds are uniform in size and feel tender but springy, similar to the texture of a hard-boiled egg white, 15–20 minutes. Let the curds settle for 5 minutes.

Partial Drain: Scoop out the whey to the level of the curds; reserve some of the whey. Using your hands, work the curds gently into a solid mass about the size of the form that you are using.

Drain and Press: Place the form on a tray or drainboard and line with the cheesecloth. Dampen the cloth and form with a bit of whey. Using your hands, lift the curd mass out of the pot and press it gently into the form. When it evenly fills the form, fold the excess cloth over the curd, set the follower on top, and press down gently. Add about 1 pound (0.5 kg) of weight. Press for 15 minutes. The room temperature during draining and pressing should be between 68–72°F (20–22°C).

Remove the weight and the follower. Then remove the wrapped cheese from the form, unwrap it, and flip it over. Rearrange the cheesecloth in the form and replace the cheese, pressing the cloth into the form along with it; the cheese should still look a bit wrinkled and the rind not yet smooth. Continue to press with only 1 pound (0.5 kg) of weight for 30 minutes more.

Repeat the steps above, flipping the cheese and rearranging it in the form; this time the rind should be smoother, but still not evenly closed. Add another 1 pound (0.5 kg) of weight

for a total of 2 pounds (1 kg) and continue to press for 60 minutes more.

Repeat the steps again; now the rind should be very even, perhaps with a few small openings. If not, you may add up to 2 pounds more weight. Continue to press for 4 hours more.

Remove the cheese from the form, cut off a tiny piece, and taste it. It should have a very mild tang and taste milky with a hint of buttermilk. If it isn't slightly tangy, press it for 1 hour more and taste again.

Salt: When you have achieved the desired tang, remove the cheese from the press and place in the container with enough room around all sides for brine. Pour the brine into the container until the cheese floats. Sprinkle a thin layer of salt on top of the cheese. Cover with the lid and let soak for 5 hours. The brine and room temperature should be cool, between 50–60°F (10–15°C).

Age Vacuum Sealed: Pat the cheese dry with paper towels. Place the rack in the tub, place a mat on the rack, and set the cheese on the mat. Put the lid on the tub and place it in a cool place (below 55°F [15°C]) or in the refrigerator or a wine cooler. Flip the cheese daily until the rind dries out a bit, 7–10 days.

Place the cheese in the vacuum-sealable bag, seal it, and place it back in the refrigerator. Check and taste the cheese weekly, making notes about the flavor and texture, if desired. You may have to vacuum more air out of the bag periodically if it loosens as the cheese shrinks.

Age for 2 months for a mild cheese, 4–6 months for medium flavor, and 1 year or more for the most complex results.

Or for Natural Rind Aging: Follow steps on page 110 and age for 2 months for a mild cheese,

4–6 months for medium flavor, and 1 year or more for the most complex results.

Variations

For a beautifully colored rind, rub the cheese with a thin paste of olive oil and finely ground paprika on day five of the drying phase, before you vacuum seal the cheese. Make a thick paste and rub it in an even, but not too thick, layer on the cheese. Continue to flip daily and massage the coating on the cheese; you shouldn't need to reapply it, but you can if it looks too thin or uneven. By the time you vacuum seal the cheese, the coating should not be too oily or pasty; if so, continue to turn and massage it daily for a few more days.

Troubleshooting

After aging for a few months the cheese becomes rounded and when cut there is an open cave in the middle and lots of splits and small holes (eyes) around it: This is called *late blowing* and occurs toward the end of aging, usually after several months. It is caused by bacteria from the *clostridium* family, which can live in pasteurized or raw milk (they are not killed during pasteurization). The cheese isn't necessarily dangerous, but its flavor will not be good. Late blowing is a sign of poor milk collection techniques (which may have also introduced other bad bacteria to the milk). Throw the cheese out (or give it to the chickens or pigs), and review the tips for choosing a good milk source in chapter 2.

See also Troubleshooting in lesson 14, page 104.

Recap

Compare the steps used to make the farmhouse cheese in the last chapter with those of the Gouda recipe. The ripening and final temperatures are identical, but it is what happens later that yields very different cheeses. The Gouda curd is cut and stirred for 15 minutes without heating, and its final temperature is achieved after removing the whey and adding very hot water. These differences create a final product that has a different mineral content and develops its acid at a different stage, and therefore has a different texture, flavor, and ability to age.

Nine-month aged vacuum-sealed cheddar and monkey cheese.

LESSON 16: FRESH SQUEAKY CHEDDAR CURDS AND TRADITIONAL CHEDDAR

Cheddar is undoubtedly one of the most popular cheeses in the world. It is only surpassed in popularity and consumption by pizza cheese, also known as low-moisture mozzarella. The cheddar most of us were raised on, though, is quite different from traditional English cheddar, also called *bandaged* or *cloth bound* cheddar, which is usually wrapped tightly in a lard or butter cheesecloth and aged. The way that most American cheddar is both made and aged make it a different, but still delicious, cheese. The curds in this recipe can be enjoyed as squeaky fresh curds, pressed into a wheel and aged, or aged to make what I call "Monkey Cheese" (after the fun, pull-apart bread called monkey bread). It's hard to beat fresh squeaky curds seasoned with basil pesto, roasted garlic, or lavender. They can be frozen and used any time as a great snack, salad or pizza topping, or party appetizer.

As convenient as curds are to have on hand, making cheddar is an all-day process. But, fortunately, you can step away for short periods of time. During this lesson, you'll learn two new techniques, *cheddaring*, which involves stacking and restacking slabs of warm curds, and *milling*, the cutting of the cheddared slabs into finger-sized pieces. Industrially made cheddar is rarely produced using these age-old techniques, but instead employs a shortcut that we'll learn in the next recipe.

What You'll Need

Milk: 2 gal. (8 L) whole milk

Culture: ¼ tsp. (0.5 g) Flora Danica (for fresh curds) or MA 4000 (for aged)

Calcium Chloride (optional): ⅜ tsp. (2 ml) calcium chloride diluted in ¼ cup (60 ml) cool water

Rennet: ⅛ tsp. (1 ml) double-strength vegetarian rennet diluted just before use in ⅛ cup (30 ml) cool, non-chlorinated water

Salt: 3 tsp. (18 g) pure salt

Equipment: Pot with lid, thermometer, ladle, colander, 1 gal. (4 L) vacuum-sealable bag and vacuum sealer (for Monkey Cheese and traditional wheel), mechanical or strap press and form (for traditional wheel)

Process in a Nutshell

Time: 6 hr. active, 4–12 mo. aging (if desired)

Steps: Heat milk, add culture, ripen, add rennet, ripen and coagulate, heat and stir curd, drain, cheddar, mill, salt, use or age

Step by Step

Heat Milk: Pour the milk into the pot, and place the pot over another pot of water on the stovetop. Heat the milk until the temperature reaches 90°F (32°C).

Add Culture: Sprinkle the culture on top of milk and let set for 3–5 minutes. Using the ladle, stir gently for 2–5 minutes.

Ripen: Maintain the temperature of the milk at 90°F (32°C), and let ripen for 30 minutes.

Add Calcium Chloride (optional): Stir in the calcium chloride, if using, and let set for 5 minutes.

Rennet: Stir the milk using an up-and-down motion with the ladle. Stop stirring briefly and pour the diluted rennet over the top of the ladle. Begin stirring again for 1 minute. Hold the ladle to the top of the milk in several spots to help still the milk.

Coagulate: Maintain the temperature of the milk at 90°F (32°C), and let the curd set until a clean break is achieved, about 45 minutes.

Cut Curd: Cut curd mass into ⅜-inch (1 cm) cubes, and let rest for 5 minutes.

Heat and Stir Curd: Heat the curds very gradually, stirring gently, to 102°F (39°C) over 30 minutes. Maintain the temperature and continue stirring gently for 45 minutes. Let the curds settle for 5 minutes.

Drain and Cheddar: Position the colander over another pot or in the sink. Carefully pour the curds into the colander and let drain. Set the colander over a pot of hot water, cover, and maintain the temperature of the curds at 95–98°F (35–37°C) for 15 minutes. Flip the curd mass over in the colander and cover again, maintaining the temperature for 15 minutes more. Repeat the steps, flipping the curd mass one more time.

After 15 minutes, remove the curd mass from the colander and cut it into two equal slabs. Replace the slabs in the colander, stacking them on top of each other. Cover and maintain

the curd temperature as above. After 15 minutes, flip each slab over and reverse the order of the stack. Continue flipping and swapping the slabs every 15 minutes until the texture of the curd resembles the texture of cooked chicken breast, about 2 hours.

Mill: Place the slabs on a cutting board and cut into approximately ½-inch-wide x 1-inch-long (1.25 cm to 2.5 cm long) strips. Place the strips back in the colander, and sprinkle with 1½ teaspoons (9 g) of the salt. Stir thoroughly and let set for about 8 minutes (this is called "mellowing"). Add the remaining 1½ teaspoons (9 g) salt, stir again, and let the curds mellow for 10 minutes more.

Finishing Variations

For fresh curds: Eat the curds plain or add seasonings such as pesto, garlic, chives, chipotle peppers, or lavender. You can even sprinkle beer on the curds and let it soak in.

For Monkey Cheese: Let the salted curds sit at room temperature, 68–72°F (20°C–22°C), in the colander, stirring hourly for 3–4 hours. Place the curds in a vacuum-sealable bag and pack to the bottom of the bag. Vacuum seal and age in the refrigerator or a wine cooler for 4 months. You can open the bag and pull a curd off when you want to taste how it is progressing.

For traditional cheddar: Place the form on a tray or drain board, line the form for the press with cheesecloth, and dampen it with a bit of whey and line with the cheesecloth. Fill the form with the curds, pressing and packing them in by hand. When all of the curds are packed into the form, fold the cloth over the top, and place the follower on top. Place the form in the press. If your press has a screw with a pressure gauge, start with 10 pounds of pressure. If you are using the strap press (see chapter 3 Presses), apply pressure just until you see a bit of white whey coming from the bottom of the form. Press for 15 minutes at room temperature, 68–72°F (20–22°C).

Increase the pressure to 20 pounds or tighten the strap until white whey again comes from the bottom of the form. Press for 15 minutes.

Release the pressure. Remove the cheese from the form, unwrap it, and flip it over. Rearrange the cheesecloth in the form and replace the cheese, pressing the cloth into the form along with it; the rind should be knobby, and you should still see the outline of all of the curds, but the mass shouldn't fall apart. If the mass starts to fall apart as you handle it, leave it in the form and increase the pressure for 15 more minutes before turning.

Increase the pressure to 30 pounds or tighten the strap very firmly; there should be a lot of resistance from the cheese without a lot of white whey coming out. Press for 1 hour more.

Repeat the steps again; the rind should be closing nicely with only small outlines of the curd. Rewrap the cheese and replace it in the press. Increase the pressure to 50 pounds or tighten the strap about as tight as you can get it and press for 12 hours or overnight.

Aging vacuum sealed: Place the cheese in the vacuum-sealable bag, seal it, and place it back in the refrigerator or wine cooler for 6–12 months. Check and taste the cheese weekly, making notes about the flavor and texture, if desired. You may have to vacuum more air out of the bag periodically if it loosens as the cheese shrinks.

Or for natural rind aging: Follow steps on page 110 and age for 4–12 months. Rub the

Fresh curds with pesto are hard to beat.

rind with butter or lard at 4, 6, and 12 weeks. For aging over 6 months, recipe size should be doubled.

Troubleshooting

Curds never get "cooked chicken-breast" texture: Continue the cheddaring process for longer. You can also try filling a zipper-lock plastic bag with 100°F (38°C) water and placing it on top of the slabs during cheddaring.

See also Troubleshooting for lessons 14 and 15.

Recap

Let's talk a bit more about the protein network in cheese. In chapter 2, you learned what rennet does when added to the milk: it changes the way the proteins behave and allows them to form a network that creates the curd. Now picture a 3-D network of interconnected fishing nets or Tinker Toys, (if you are old enough to have played with those). Now, think of that as we talk about the two different ways we manipulate cheese.

When we make mozzarella, we form a network that is able to stretch. We do that by using a combination of just the right amount of acid and the heat of the whey. When first working the curd, that 3-D network doesn't want to stretch, but by slowly manipulating it, we are able to rearrange the strands so that they line up better and become elastic.

When we make cheddar, we do something similar, but we use time and the pressure of the stacked slabs to slowly realign the network. When finished cheddaring, we can see the changed structure in the cooked chicken-breast texture. Both mozzarella and cheddar are what are called "texturized" cheeses, meaning that the cheesemaker has purposefully created a different texture in the cheese. When you bite into a fresh cheddar curd, it's the wet, slick protein network sliding against your smooth teeth that causes the squeak.

BONUS RECIPE: TWO-HOUR CHEDDAR CURDS

What You'll need:

Milk: 1 gallon (4 L)

Culture: 1 cup fresh, cultured buttermilk (if purchased, buy one with the longest expiration date to ensure that the bacteria are still active)

Rennet: ¼ tsp.(1.25 ml) double strength (or ½ tsp (2.5 ml) single strength)

Utensils: Pot, thermometer, ladle, knife, colander, zipperlock bag

Steps:

Heat milk and add culture: Combine milk and buttermilk in a stainless steel pot. Place on direct heat and warm, stirring constantly to 95°F. Turn off or remove from heat.

Add rennet: Diluted in 2 TB (30 ml) cool non chlorinated water and stir into milk with 5 up and down strokes.

Coagulate: Let set for 10–15 minutes until just pulling away from the sides or firm when pulled away

Cut and Stir Curd: Cut into ⅜ to ¼ inch pieces then let rest for 5 minutes. Stir very gently for 5 minutes at 95°F. Begin to increase heat very slowly over 15 minutes to reach 102°F

Drain: Pour curds into cloth lined colander and tie in a bundle. Cover and keep curd at 100 F for 10 minutes

Cheddar: Cut slab into two pieces, stack, cover and keep warm, use a plastic bag filled with 100°F hot water to help keep the curd slabs warm. Turn every 10 minutes until chicken breast texture is achieved (about 1 hour)

Mill: Cut slabs into ½ to 1 inch (1–2 cm) long by ¼ to ½ inch (½ – 1 cm) wide pieces.

Salt: Place in colander over hot whey and sprinkle with ½ tsp salt. Stir then cover with hot water bag for 5 min. (mellowing) Repeat salting and mellowing one more time.

Use: Curds are ready to eat as soon as they are done.

LESSON 17: STIRRED-CURD CHEDDAR

In this recipe, we'll learn another new technique: stirring the curd in the pot after the whey has been removed. During this step, the curd continues to ripen and drain. As with traditional cheddar, the curd is salted and then pressed. The result is a cheese very similar to traditional cheddar, but made in a much shorter time. Many industrially made cheddars use this method, both as a way of shortening production and because it can be adapted to work in enclosed cheddar-making equipment. The biggest disappointment of this recipe when compared to the other is that you don't end up with squeaky fresh curds!

What You'll Need

Milk: 2 gal. (8 L) whole milk

Culture: ¼ tsp. (0.5 g) MA 4000

Calcium Chloride (optional): ⅜ tsp. (2 ml) calcium chloride diluted in ¼ cup (60 ml) cool water

Rennet: ⅛ tsp. (1 ml) double-strength vegetarian rennet diluted just before use in ⅛ cup (30 ml) cool, non-chlorinated water

Annatto (optional): 2 drops diluted in ⅛ cup (30 ml) water

Salt: 3 tsp. (18 g) pure salt

Equipment: 2 pots, thermometer, ladle, colander, cheesecloth, tray or drainboard, mechanical or strap press and form, 1 gal. (4 L) vacuum-sealable bag and vacuum sealer

Process in a Nutshell

Time: 4–5 hr. active, 14 hours inactive (pressing), 4–12 mo. aging

Steps: Heat milk, add culture, ripen, add rennet, ripen and coagulate, cut curd, heat and stir curd, drain and stir curd, salt, press, age

Step by Step

Heat Milk: Pour the milk into the pot, and place the pot over another pot of water on the stovetop. Heat the milk until the temperature reaches 90°F (32°C).

Add Culture: Sprinkle the culture on top of milk and let set for 3–5 minutes. Using the ladle, stir gently for 2–5 minutes.

Ripen: Maintain the temperature of the milk at 90°F (32°C), and let ripen for 60 minutes.

Add Calcium Chloride: Stir in calcium chloride solution, if using, and let set for 5 minutes.

Add Rennet: Stir the milk using an up-and-down motion with the ladle. Stop stirring briefly and pour the diluted rennet over the top of the ladle. Begin stirring again for 1 minute. Hold the ladle to the top of the milk in several spots to help still the milk.

Coagulate: Maintain the temperature of the milk at 90°F (32°C), and let the curd set until a clean break is achieved, about 45 minutes.

Cut Curd: Cut curd mass into ⅜-inch (1 cm) cubes, and let rest for 5 minutes.

Heat and Stir Curd: Heat the curds very gradually, stirring gently, to 101°F (39°C) over 45 minutes. Maintain the temperature and continue stirring every few minutes for 60 minutes. Let the curds settle for 5 minutes.

Drain and Stir Curd: Pour the curds into a colander and then return them to the pot. Stir the curds, maintaining the curd temperature at 95–96°F (35 to 36°C) for 30 minutes. Position the colander over another pot or in the sink.

Annatto-colored stirred curd cheddar ready for vacuum sealing and aging.

Carefully pour the curds into the colander and let drain.

Salt: Set the colander over a pot of hot water and sprinkle with 1½ teaspoons (9 g) of the salt. Stir thoroughly and let set for 10 minutes. Add the remaining 1½ teaspoons (9 g) salt, stir again, and let the curds mellow for 20 minutes more.

Press: Line the form for the press with cheesecloth and dampen it with a bit of whey. Fill the form with the curds, pressing and packing them in by hand. When all of the curds are packed into the form, fold the cloth over the top, and place the follower on top. Place the form in the press. If your press has a screw with a pressure gauge, start with 10 pounds of pressure. If you are using the strap press, apply pressure just until you see a bit of white whey coming from the bottom of the form. Press for 15 minutes at room temperature, 68–72°F (20–22°C).

Increase the pressure to 20 pounds or tighten the strap until white whey again comes from the bottom of the form. Press for 15 minutes.

Release the pressure. Remove the cheese from the form, unwrap it, and flip it over. Rearrange the cheesecloth in the form and replace the cheese, pressing the cloth into the form along with it; the rind should be knobby, and you should still see the outline of all of the curds, but the mass shouldn't fall apart. If the mass starts to fall apart as you handle it, leave it in the form and increase the pressure for 15 more minutes before turning.

Increase the pressure to 30 pounds or tighten the strap very firmly; there should be a lot of resistance from the cheese without a lot of white whey coming out. Press for 1 hour more.

Repeat the steps again; the rind should be closing nicely with only small outlines of the curd. Rewrap the cheese and replace it in the press. Increase the pressure to 50 pounds or tighten the strap about as tight as you can get it and press for 12 hours or overnight.

Age Vacuum Sealed: Place the cheese in the vacuum-sealable bag, seal it, and place it back in the refrigerator for 4–12 months. Check and taste the cheese weekly, making notes about the flavor and texture, if desired. You may have to vacuum more air out of the bag periodically if it loosens as the cheese shrinks.

Or for Natural Rind Aging: Follow steps on page 110 and age for 4–12 months. For aging over 6 months, recipe size should be doubled.

Troubleshooting

See Troubleshooting for lessons 14 and 15, pages 104, 115.

Recap

If possible, try to make a wheel of both the traditional cheddar and the stirred curd cheddar at about the same time. Then age them both and compare the flavor and texture at different times throughout the aging. You should notice that the texture of the traditional wheel is a bit denser and that of the stirred curd a bit more crumbly. This is because the protein network made using the stirred curd method isn't as reshaped and texturized as the one made with the traditional cheddar method. Even though the texture of the cheeses is a bit different, when aged for similar amounts of time, their flavors should be quite similar.

This wheel of Colby was made using goat's milk and was aged at 55F (12C) for 30 days in a tub. The molds on the rind had no negative affect on the flavor, which was creamy and quite complex for its age.

LESSON 18: COLBY

Now for the ultimate combination of techniques: stirring the curd and washing the curd. Colby is a bit like a stirred-curd cheddar, but its final texture and flavor are unique because the curd is also washed. The washing step is similar to the one we used when making Gouda earlier, but instead of hot water, we'll be using cold. The resulting cheese should be reminiscent of cheddar, but with a milder flavor and more pliable, tender texture. Like Monterey Jack, Colby is an American original created in Colby, Wisconsin in the late 1880's.

What You'll Need

Milk: 2 gal. (8 L) whole milk

Culture: ¼ tsp. (0.4 g) MA 4000

Calcium Chloride (optional): ¼ tsp. (1.5 ml) calcium chloride diluted in ⅛ cup (30 ml) cool water

Rennet: ⅛ tsp. (1.5 ml) double-strength vegetarian rennet diluted just before use in ⅛ cool, non-chlorinated water

Salt: 2 tsp. (10 g) pure salt

Equipment: 2 pots, thermometer, ladle, colander, pot with lid, cheesecloth, tray or drainboard, mechanical or strap press and form, 1 gal. (4 L) vacuum-sealable bag and vacuum sealer

Process in a Nutshell

Time: 3½ hr. active, 12 hr. inactive, 2–4 mo. aging

Steps: Heat milk, add culture, ripen, add rennet, ripen and coagulate, cut curd, heat and stir curd, partial drain, wash, stir and drain, stir, salt, press, store and use

Step by Step

Heat Milk: Pour the milk into the pot, and place the pot over another pot of water on the stovetop. Heat the milk until the temperature reaches 88–90°F (31–32°C).

Add Culture: Sprinkle the culture on top of milk and let set for 3–5 minutes. Using the ladle, stir gently for 2–5 minutes.

Ripen: Maintain the temperature of the milk at 88–90°F (31–32°C), stirring occasionally, for 40 minutes.

Add Calcium Chloride (optional): Stir in the calcium chloride, if using, and let set for 5 minutes.

Add the Rennet: Stir the milk using an up-and-down motion with the ladle. Stop stirring briefly and pour the diluted rennet over the top of the ladle. Begin stirring again for 1 minute. Hold the ladle to the top of the milk in several spots to help still the milk.

Coagulate: Maintain the temperature of the milk at 88–90°F (31–32°C), and let the curd set until a clean break is achieved, about 45 minutes.

Cut Curd: Cut the curd mass into ⅜-inch (1 cm) cubes, and let rest for 5 minutes.

Heat and Stir Curd: Heat the curds very gradually, stirring gently, to 102°F (39°C) over 45 minutes. Maintain the temperature of the curds at 102°F (39°C) and stir for 15 minutes. Let the curds settle for 15–30 minutes.

Partial Drain: Scoop out the whey to 1 inch (2.5 cm) above the curds.

Wash Curd: Stir the curds and slowly add cold tap water (about 60°F [16°C]) until the temperature of the whey reaches 80–86°F (27–30°C). Maintain the temperature and stir for 15 minutes more.

Drain and Stir Curd: Scoop out the whey to the level of curds, and stir for 10 minutes. Position the colander over another pot and carefully pour the curds into the colander and let drain, reserve the whey. Set the colander over a pot of hot water and stir the curd with your hands for 20 minutes, maintaining the temperature of the curds at 80–86°F (27–30°C). Taste the curds; they should be sweet and mild.

Salt: Sprinkle the curds with 1 teaspoon (6 g) of the salt and stir well; the whey coming from the curds will become milky white. Cover the colander and let the curds set for 5–10 minutes. Add the remaining 1 teaspoon (6 g) salt, stir again, and let the curds mellow for 5–10 minutes more.

Press: Place the form on a tray or drainboard, line the form for the press with cheesecloth, and dampen it with a bit of whey. Fill the form with the curds, pressing and packing them in by hand. When all of the curds are packed into the form, fold the cloth over the top, and place the follower on top. Place the form in the press. If your press has a screw with a pressure gauge, start with 10 pounds of pressure. If you are using the strap press, apply pressure just until you see a bit of white whey coming from the bottom of the form. Press for 15 minutes, maintaining room temperature, 68°F–72°F (20°C–22°C), if possible.

Increase the pressure to 20 pounds or tighten the strap until white whey again comes from the bottom of the form. Press for 15 minutes.

Release the pressure and remove the follower. Remove the cheese from the form, unwrap it, and flip it over. Rearrange the cheesecloth in the form, and then replace the cheese, pressing the cloth into the form along with it; the rind should be knobby, and you should still see the outline of all of the curds, but the mass shouldn't fall apart. If the mass starts to fall apart as you handle it, leave it in the form and increase the pressure for 15 more minutes before turning.

Replace the follower and increase the pressure to 30 pounds or tighten the strap very firmly; there should be a lot of resistance from the cheese without a lot of white whey coming out. Press for 1 hour more.

Repeat the steps again; the rind should be closing nicely with only small outlines of the curd. Rewrap the cheese and replace it in the press. Replace the follower and increase the pressure to 50 pounds or tighten the strap about as tight as you can get it and press for 12 hours or overnight.

Age Vacuum Sealed: Place the cheese in the vacuum-sealable bag, seal it, and place it back in the refrigerator for 2–3 months. Check and taste the cheese weekly, making notes about the flavor and texture, if desired. You may have to vacuum more air out of the bag periodically if it loosens as the cheese shrinks.

Or for Natural Rind Aging: Follow steps on page 110 and age for 2–3 months.

Troubleshooting

See Troubleshooting lessons 14 and 15, page 104, 115.

Recap

You might be wondering how the difference in water temperature of the washed Gouda curds and the washed Colby curds changed the cheeses. In both cases, the removal of whey and its replacement with water helped make the cheese a little more pliable. In the case of Gouda, the hot water helped shrink and cook the curds. In the Colby lesson, the warm curds actually absorbed some of the cooler water and increased the moisture inside the curds so that rather than shrinking them, the water plumps them. This leads to a cheese with a different milder texture and flavor, but one that isn't a good candidate for long aging. Because the acid content is a little lower and the moisture content a bit higher than many other cheeses, Colby is usually made from pasteurized milk (remember it is acid that keeps the unwanted microbes from growing). I find it interesting that a cheese like Colby that is considered simple actually involves more steps than some other cheeses that age into super-complex delights.

Pholia Farm's Covered Bridge cheese uses the Colby recipe but includes an added step during draining and stirring the curds. A dark ale is added to the curds, giving a wonderful flavor to the aged cheese. The beer bottle shape was embossed into the cheese by making a cutout form from a thin, plastic cutting board and the date was carved into the cheese by hand.

LESSON 19: PARMESAN

Now it's time to try your hand at making a cheese using a different type of culture and higher temperatures than any of the other rennet-coagulated cheeses we have made so far. Most high-heat cheeses age for long periods of time and are hard in texture, very complex in flavor, and Italian in origin. The cheeses in this group are sometimes called *grana*, which is Italian for grain. It refers to the tiny curds that are formed during their making and the granular texture of the cheeses when they are cut. Members of this family include the exquisite Parmigiano-Reggiano and Grana Padano. The name "Parmesan" is currently used to describe a number of cheeses that are similar, but not strictly defined. I say "currently" because the Italians are hard at work hoping to protect the identity of their cheese traditions by having the name legally defined. Pecorino Romano, which is made with sheep's instead of cow's milk, is much different in texture, thanks to its high fat content, but otherwise similar.

For this recipe, I recommend that you use milk lower in fat than whole milk if you are trying to emulate traditional Parmesan, as it is made with cow's milk that has had much of the fat removed. This doesn't make the cheese dry, though, because during aging the proteins break down and create a wonderful texture. You can use any milk, but your results will be different. Hopefully by now you are not too surprised at this and possibly even enjoying the unpredictability of each recipe and type of milk.

What You'll Need

Milk: 2 gal. (8 L) partly skimmed milk (2–2.8% fat)

Culture: ¼ tsp. (0.5 g) Thermo B

Calcium Chloride (optional): ¼ tsp. (1.25 ml) calcium chloride diluted in ¼ cup (30 ml) cool water

Rennet: ¼ tsp. (1.25 ml) double-strength vegetarian rennet diluted just before use in ¼ cup (30 ml) cool, non-chlorinated water

Salt: Heavy brine (recipe in chapter 4) and pure salt

Utensils: Pot, thermometer, ladle, colander, cheesecloth, tray, mechanical or strap press and form, 1 gal. (4 L) vacuum-sealable bag and vacuum sealer

Process in a Nutshell

Time: 2½ hr. active, 11–17 hr. inactive, 4–12 mo. aging

Steps: Heat milk, add culture, ripen, add rennet, ripen and coagulate, cut and stir curd, heat and stir curd, drain and press, salt, age, store and use

Step by Step

Heat Milk: Pour the milk into the pot, and place the pot over another pot of water on the stovetop. Heat the milk until the temperature reaches 88–90°F (31–32°C).

Add Culture: Sprinkle the culture on top of

milk and let set for 3–5 minutes. Using the ladle, stir gently for 2–5 minutes.

Add Calcium Chloride (optional): Stir in the calcium chloride, if using, and let set for 5 minutes.

Add rennet: Stir the milk using an up-and-down motion with the ladle. Stop stirring briefly and pour the diluted rennet over the top of the ladle. Begin stirring again for 1 minute. Hold the ladle to the top of the milk in several spots to help still the milk.

Coagulate: Maintain the temperature of the milk at 88–90°F (31–32°C), and let the curd set until a clean break is achieved, about 30 minutes.

Cut and Stir Curd: Slowly cut the curd mass into ¼-inch (6 mm) cubes over 10 minutes while maintaining the temperature at 88–90°F (31–32°C). Maintain the temperature of the curds and stir gently for 10–15 minutes.

Heat and Stir Curd: Heat the curds very gradually, stirring gently, to 108°F (42°C) over 30 minutes. Maintain the temperature and stir for 5 minutes. Continue stirring and increase the temperature of the curds to 124°F–128°F (51°C–53°C) over 30 minutes. Let settle for 5 minutes.

Drain and Press: Place the form on a tray or drainboard, line the form for the press with cheesecloth, and dampen it with a bit of whey

This beautiful Parmesan-style cheese made by Ian Treuer was aged vacuum sealed for 14 months. It shows the desired grain, or grana, texture typical of a classic Italian cheese. PHOTO BY AND COURTESY OF IAN TREUER

and line with the cheesecloth. Fill the form with the curds, pressing and packing them in by hand. When all of the curds are packed into the form, fold the cloth over the top, and place the follower on top. Place the form in the press. If your press has a screw with a pressure gauge, start with 10 pounds of pressure. If you are using the strap press (see chapter 3 Presses), apply pressure just until you see a bit of white whey coming from the bottom of the form. Press for 15 minutes. The room temperature during draining and pressing should be 68–72°F (20–22°C).

Increase the pressure to 20 pounds or tighten the strap until white whey again comes from the bottom of the form. Press for 15 minutes.

Release the pressure. Remove the cheese from the form, unwrap it, and flip it over. Rearrange the cheesecloth in the form and replace the cheese, pressing the cloth into the form along with it; the rind should be knobby, and you should still see the outline of all of the curds, but the mass shouldn't fall apart. If the mass starts to fall apart as you handle it, leave it in the form and increase the pressure for 15 more minutes before turning.

Increase the pressure to 30 pounds or tighten the strap very firmly; there should be a lot of resistance from the cheese without a lot of white whey coming out. Press for 1 hour more.

Repeat the steps again; the rind should be closing nicely with only small outlines of the curd. Rewrap the cheese and replace it in the press. Increase the pressure to 50 pounds or tighten the strap about as tight as you can get it and press for 12 hours or overnight.

Remove the cheese from the form, cut off a tiny piece, and taste it. It should have a very mild tang and taste milky with a hint of buttermilk. If it isn't slightly tangy, press it for 1 hour more and taste it again.

Salt: When you have achieved the desired tang, remove the cheese from the press and place in the container with enough room around all sides for brine. Pour the brine into the container until the cheese floats. Sprinkle a thin layer of salt on top of the cheese. Cover with the lid and let soak for 10 hours. The brine and room temperature should be cool, between 50–60°F (10–15°C).

Age Vacuum Sealed: Pat the cheese dry with paper towels. Place the rack in the tub, place a mat on the rack, and set the cheese on the mat. Put the lid on the tub and place it in a cool place (below 55°F [15°C]) or in the refrigerator or a wine cooler. Flip the cheese daily until the rind dries out a bit, 7–10 days.

Place the cheese in the vacuum-sealable bag, seal it, and place it back in the refrigerator or wine cooler. Check and taste the cheese weekly, making notes about the flavor and texture, if desired. You may have to vacuum more air out of the bag periodically if it loosens as the cheese shrinks.

Age for 4–6 months for a mild cheese and 1 year or more for the most complex results.

Or for Natural Rind Aging: Follow steps on page 110. Rub with a light coat of olive oil at 3 weeks, 6 weeks, and 12 weeks of age and age for 4–6 months for a mild cheese, a year for the most complex results. For aging over 6 months, recipe size should be doubled.

Troubleshooting

Cracks in cheese during brining or aging: Because the curds in grana-style cheeses are so small and dry, it can take a lot of pressure to properly knit them back together. Also, make sure that the room doesn't cool below the suggested temperature during pressing; warmth will help the curds to knit back together.

See also Troubleshooting in lessons 14 and 15.

Recap

Let's first compare the amount of rennet used in this recipe to all of the others in this chapter: we used twice as much in this recipe, but the same amount of milk. This is one reason that the coagulation time was only 30 minutes instead of 45 minutes. But the main reason for the shorter coagulation has to do with the amount of protein in the milk. When you use partly skimmed milk, there is less fat in the milk. Less fat, by default, means more protein. During aging, these proteins need a few more enzymes to help them break down; the rennet provides these enzymes.

BONUS RECIPE: WHEY RICOTTA

Let's tie things together by returning to our first cheese, ricotta, but instead making pure whey ricotta with no added milk or acid. This is truly what ricotta was meant to be: recooked (remember that is what the word ricotta means) whey that produced a curd of tender whey proteins that could be used for cooking. Whey ricotta is a rare thing today; instead, more often the whey is heated and a portion of milk is added to increase the total yield. You can do that too, but why not try it first the way it was intended?

What You'll Need

Fresh Whey: Any amount from making any of the cheeses in this chapter

Equipment: Pot, thermometer, ladle, cheesecloth-lined sieve

Process in a Nutshell

Time: 15–20 minutes active.

Step by Step

Heat Whey: Pour the whey into the pot and place the pot over high heat. Heat the whey, stirring only occasionally (it won't burn), until you see tiny white flecks floating to the surface; this usually happens at 175–185°F (79–85°C).

Drain: Remove the pot from the heat and let set for about 10 minutes. Position the sieve over another pot or in the sink. Using the ladle, skim as much of the curd as you can and pour it into the sieve. Skimming, instead of pouring, helps keep the delicate curd from breaking up. Let the curds drain for about 15 minutes.

Chill: Transfer the curds to a container, cover, and chill.

Store and Use: Store the ricotta in the refrigerator for up to 7 days. Use for desserts or in cooking. There isn't much of a yield, but it is such a unique cheese and such a great example of how heat affects the milk proteins that it is a must for those learning cheesemaking.

Adding milk to the whey to increase yield and change texture (optional).

Whey ricotta being scooped from the surface of the hot whey.

9: WHAT'S NEXT?

I WAS VERY TEMPTED TO INCLUDE a few recipes for some trickier but wonderful cheeses in this book. A Brie-type with its fluffy, white, mushroom-scented rind; a stinky, sticky washed-rind cheese; and a pungent, umami-endowed blue cheese were on my list of recipes to cover. But as I started working on them, I was reminded of how truly complex and unique their processes are — they are not basic cheeses. Each of these categories of cheeses involves some distinctive steps that rely on understanding some fairly advanced cheese chemistry if you really want to ensure consistent success. So what do we do next? Here are my recommendations on what to do if you have really enjoyed yourself thus far.

KEEP A CHEESE JOURNAL

Every good cheesemaker can follow a recipe, but every great cheesemaker keeps a detailed record of every cheese they make. Your cheese journal

Just a few of my cheese journals from over the years.

can include minimal information, or it can be as detailed as your obsessive-compulsive heart desires. The journal will be your only source for looking back and troubleshooting for possible reasons that a cheese didn't turn out — or your only source for duplicating a happy accident! Here are some ideas for record keeping:

- Make a copy of the recipe and attach it to the journal pages, or write all of the steps down right in the journal.
- Note the type of milk, its age, and the source (grocery store, farm, etc.).
- Include the time that each step was performed plus the actual measurements of culture, rennet, etc., and the type of culture and rennet used (if it varies from the recipe).
- Include the actual temperatures of the milk and curd throughout the process.
- Include the room temperature during draining and pressing.
- Make notes that describe the texture, aroma, and flavor of the cheese (even describing the milk flavor is helpful).
- If the cheese is aged, keep careful notes of aging times, temperatures, and how the cheese looks throughout the process.
- If the cheese is aged, open the bag at several points during aging, taste the cheese, make a note in your journal about the texture and flavor, and then reseal the cheese — unless you decide that it is ready to eat!

EXPERIMENT

Repeat any recipes that you particularly enjoyed making, but vary the type of milk used. Try other experiments using different cultures and even different rennets. Compare your notes (in your well-kept journal) and see if you can figure out how the change altered the cheese. I highly recommend not making more than one change for each experiment so that you can identify which element caused the change.

ADVANCED CHEESEMAKING

It won't take long for you to outgrow this book — and that's the idea! You may simply want to move on to a greater selection of recipes, or you may want to dig below the surface of beginning-level science. When you are ready to learn more complicated techniques and much deeper cheese science, I hope that my book *Mastering Artisan Cheesemaking* will be the answer to your thirst for cheesy knowledge. There are many other wonderful books available, see the appendix for a list of some of my favorites, as well, not to mention cheesemaking classes and videos. The popularity of the topic is inspiring.

CHEESEMAKING AS A BUSINESS

If you share the results of your hobby with your friends, neighbors, and coworkers, it won't be long before you start hearing things like "I would buy this!" "I know a chef who would go crazy for this cheese!" or "You should sell this in stores!" As a part of your cheesemaking journey, you might visit a farmstead creamery; see the lush pastures, adorable animals, and hardworking farmers; and perhaps begin feeling a little wistful for such a life. (I speak of these things from personal experience.) If the siren song of cheesemaker does begin to resonate in your heart, then you may be about to depart on a new journey, but (also speaking from experience) it is only one to be pursued after an exhaustive amount of research and even work-study.

Cheesemaking as a business is rarely a profitable type of enterprise — unless it is on a large scale. Most small-scale cheesemaking businesses are what are considered "lifestyle businesses." In other words, the lifestyle itself is the goal, not investment and large profit. Most small cheese businesses rely upon another source of income or benefits (such as health care from a retirement or second job) to help make ends meet. The life itself is exhausting and precarious — but don't get me wrong, there are many joys and rewards, but these are much easier to see from the outside and can lead to the illusion of a far different lifestyle than is the reality.

The Small-Scale Cheese Business and *The Small-Scale Dairy,* two of my other books, were written to help you better understand the career and make the right decisions — even if one of those decisions is to NOT become a licensed cheesemaker.

CONCLUSION

I hope that by the end of this book you are even more excited about cheesemaking than you were at the beginning. I can't tell you how much more there is to learn, but I can tell you that each new piece of knowledge and each new challenge has been incredibly stimulating and fulfilling for me. Making cheese never gets old, as long as you remain humble and ready to learn. I wish you many happy hours stirring the curd and — dare I say it — cutting the cheese!

Acid/Acidic. A substance with a pH below neutral 7. Flavors associated with acid are sour, tart, and tangy.

Affinage. The French term, now widely used, for the care and tending of cheese during aging.

Annato. Natural orange coloring used in cheese. Made from the seeds of pods from a tropical and subtropical tree called the achiote.

Artisan. In cheesemaking, the term can mean the production of cheese by hand or a small company that produces cheese by hand.

Bandaged. A cheese whose rind has been encased by a thin layer of fat-soaked cheesecloth and aged. Also called "clothbound." Traditional treatment for cheddar.

Blowing. Applies to unwanted gas production within the curd or cheese that leads to the expansion of the mass. "**Early blowing**" occurs just after production and is usually caused by bacteria from the coliform family and yeasts. "**Late blowing**" occurs toward the end of aging, usually several months later, and is caused by bacteria from the *clostridium* family or propionic acid bacteria.

Brine. A saltwater solution in which cheeses are floated after pressing to provide them with salt. Also the act of salting a cheese in brine.

Butter muslin. Finely woven cloth for draining dairy products with small particles. Cheesecloth with a thread count of 90 threads per square inch is often called butter muslin.

Butterfat. Term used to describe the fat, or lipids, in milk. Butterfat and cream are similar but not exactly interchangeable.

Calcium. Mineral salt in milk. Exists alone and bound to other minerals. Plays a key role in coagulation and finished texture of cheese.

Calcium chloride. Food-grade additive used in milk to assist with coagulation and in brine to create a mineral balance, or equilibrium, between the cheese and the brine solution.

Cheddar. Refers both to a cheese type and to the process of cheddaring, in which cooked curd is drained and allowed to mat together for an extended period. Slabs of curd are usually turned and restacked several times during the cheddaring process.

Cheesecloth. A fabric with an open weave that traps curd within but allows whey to drain. Can be made of natural fabrics (often linen, also called muslin) or synthetic. Comes in various weave consistencies, or thread counts.

Chymosin. Enzyme produced in young **ruminants**' stomachs (abomasum) and used to coagulate milk for cheesemaking. Is also produced through the fermentation of genetically engineered microorganisms.

Clean break. Describes the behavior of coagulated milk when a tool is used to lift the curd and observe how it separates, or breaks. A clean break is free from jagged tears, and the whey that drains from the break is not whitish.

Clostridium. *Clostridium tyrobutyricum* microorganism responsible for forming eyes, splits, and opening in aged cheeses, referred to as "late blowing."

Coagulant. Ingredient added to milk to cause it to thicken. Coagulants include animal sources such as chymosin and pepsin (rennet), microbial sources such as *Mucor miehei* (vegetarian rennet) and fermented chymosin (also vegetarian), and plant sources such as cardoon thistle.

Coagulate. The act and process of adding coagulant. Synonymous with "curdle" and "set."

Coliforms. A large group of bacteria associated with fecal matter. Can ferment milk sugar and create gas, called "early blowing" in cheeses. There are several variations of *E. coli* that can cause severe illness and even death.

Components. Refers to the constituents within milk such as fat, protein, lactose, and calcium.

Creaming. The behavior of non-homogenized milk that causes fat to separate and float or "cream."

Cream-top. Describes milk that has not been homogenized, or products such as yogurt made from such milk and that therefore experience a degree of separation of the cream even after production.

Culture (noun). Bacteria and other microorganisms added to milk to produce changes, such as acid development. *Starter culture* refers to bacteria added whose primary job is the production of acid. *Ripening culture,* also called *adjunct* or *secondary,* is used to provide microorganisms that will facilitate changes during ripening or aging.

Culture (verb). The process of introducing microorganisms into a substance where they will grow. Synonymous in cheesemaking with innoculate.

Curd. Refers to pieces of coagulated milk cut by the cheesemaker, the final product of cottage cheese, and the milled pieces of fresh cheddar cheese.

Curdle. See **Coagulate.**

Dry salt. Term used to describe the act of salting a cheese by adding dry salt to the curd or to the surface of a pressed wheel.

Early blowing. See **Blowing.**

Enzyme. A substance that causes biochemical reactions to occur or occur more rapidly.

Eyes. Openings in cheese present either because of the lightness of pressing — leaving openings — or the formation of gas in the paste after pressing.

Farmstead. A cheesemaking operation using only the milk of its own animals to produce cheese on the farm.

Fermentation. The breakdown of a substance that produces acid and other by-products such as carbon dioxide. Usually associated with the breakdown of sugars (carbohydrates).

Follower. The portion of a cheese press or form that sits atop the cheese and evenly distributes the pressing weight. Named because it "follows" the cheese as it shrinks and is pressed.

Globule. Small spherical mass, such as how milk fat exists in milk.

Homogenization. Mechanical treatment of milk in which fat globules are reduced in size and cryoglobulin (a protein that encourages milk to cream) is denatured, resulting in fat that doesn't separate from the milk.

Junket rennet. Coagulant made using enzymes from an adult ruminant's stomach (abomasum). Consists mostly of pepsin. Not a good choice for cheesemaking, as pepsin will break down proteins too rapidly after coagulation.

Kosher salt. Flaked salt. Comes in "additive-free" or "with anti-caking agents" versions.

Lactase. Enzyme that breaks lactose into its two simple sugars, glucose and galactose. Some individuals do not produce lactase in their digestive tracts and are therefore lactose intolerant.

Lactose. Double sugar (disaccharide) sugar in milk comprising two simple sugars, glucose and galactose.

Late blowing. See **Blowing.**

Lipase. Enzyme that breaks down fats (lipids). Naturally present in milk and gastric system of animals. Commercially available and can be added to cheese milk to increase fat breakdown and flavor.

Mellowing. Refers to the time after the salting of milled curds when the salt is allowed to dissolve and be partly absorbed by the curd.

Mesophilic. Category of bacteria that prefer a warm temperature range of 80°F–102°F (27°C– 39°C).

Microbial rennet. Enzymatic coagulant produced by microbes. Most common microbe used is *Rhizomucor miehei.*

Microorganism. Refers to all microscopic life, such as bacteria, viruses, and fungi (yeasts and molds).

Mill. The act of cutting or breaking curds that have been compacted (and usually cheddared) into smaller pieces.

Mold. Refers to both a form in which cheese is drained and a member of a group of fungi.

Nonreactive. Indicates a material, in cheesemaking a pot or utensil, that will not erode or degrade in the presence of other substances, such as milk. Many metals, such as aluminum, will react with the acid produced by cheesemaking.

Pasteurization. Heat treatment designed to destroy or limit major food-borne pathogens. Legally defined and must conform to specific temperatures and times.

Pathogen. A disease- or illness-causing microorganism.

Piquant. Peppery or sharp, usually used to describe aged cheeses where lipase has played a role in the breakdown of fats, helping to create this flavor sensation.

Protease. Any enzyme that breaks down proteins. Sometimes called proteinase.

Protein. One or more strands of polypeptides (long chains of amino acids). Source of nutrition for living things. Milk protein — caseins and whey proteins — exists in a micellar form suspended in the liquid and within the liquid portion.

Pure salt. Sodium chloride without any additives such as iodine (commonly added to table salt) or anti-caking substances.

Rennet. More properly refers to animal-source coagulant but now commonly used to mean any enzymatic coagulant. See also **Coagulant.**

Ruminant. An animal that has a compartmented upper digestive system (usually with four chambers), including a rumen. Ruminants regurgitate matter from the rumen and "chew a cud."

Sanitize. To remove microorganisms from an object, usually through heat or chemicals used after cleaning. A sanitized object may or may not be considered *sterilized* — having no life forms — depending on the treatment used.

Slime compounds. Compounds produced by some bacteria, resulting in a viscous, slimy texture. Found in some yogurt cultures and sometimes seen in cheese brine.

Starter culture. Bacterial culture added at the start of the cheesemaking process to acidify the milk.

Sterilize. Techniques and processes by which all living matter is removed or destroyed on a surface or implement.

Stirred curd. Term describing cheeses made using a technique in which the drained cheese curd is stirred for a period of time in the warm vat.

Terroir. French term meaning "a sense of place or locality." Used to describe characteristics imparted to the milk and cheese from local conditions, food sources, aging environment, and so on.

Thermization. Process of heat treating milk at temperatures and times not defined by the regulations regarding legal pasteurization; destroys some bacteria.

Thermophilic. Heat-loving bacterium that grows well at temperatures of approximately 100°F–120°F (38°C–49°C). Most often used in Italian-style cheeses.

Ultra-high temperature. Milk that has been heat treated to 280°F (138°C) for 2 seconds. Does not need refrigeration and is not suitable for cheesemaking. Also known as UHT milk.

Ultra-pasteurized. Milk that has been heat treated to 240°F (116°C) for 4–15 seconds. Not suitable for cheesemaking. Also known as UP milk.

Washed curd. Technique in which whey is removed from the vat during the cooking process and replaced with water or a light brine. Decreases acid production during cooking by removing a portion of lactose.

Water bath. Describes the use of a double-walled or two-part container in which the outer portion contains hot water that heats the contents of the interior container.

Whey. Liquid watery portion of milk separated during cheesemaking; contains lactose, starter bacteria, whey proteins, and water-soluble vitamins.

Yield. The amount of cheese obtained in comparison to the amount of milk used. Can also refer to the amount of milk produced by a dairy animal.

Books

Cheese Primer by Steve Jenkins (Workman, 1996)

This was my first cheese book, a gift from friends. What it lacks in glamour and color photos, it makes up for with insight and depth. Steve is an icon in the cheese world for good reason.

The Cheesemaker's Manual, by Margaret Morris (Glengarry Cheese Making Supply, 2003)

From the owner of Glengarry Cheese Making supply in Canada. A great reference and resource.

The Fabrication of Farmstead Goat Cheese by Jean-Claude Le Jaouen (The Cheesemakers Journal, 1987)

If you plan on making any mold-ripened cheeses — cow, goat, or sheep — you should eventually pick up this little book. Nothing else quite comes close to covering French bloomy rinded cheeses. You will learn a lot about their production, and the back includes a long list, along with details, about many of the classic French mold-ripened goat cheeses (you can make them with other milks, too, though).

Mastering Artisan Cheesemaking, by Gianaclis Caldwell (Chelsea Green Publishing, 2012)

When you are ready for a deeper look at cheesemaking and some more complicated recipes.

Mastering Cheese by Max McCalman and David Gibbons (Clarkson Potter, 2009)

This book is the brave and thorough work of one of cheese's first "celebrity" advocates. McCalman and Gibbons have two other books on cheese that are worth owning as well, but if you can only have one, get this one. The book is designed for the consumer of cheese, and I contend that cheesemakers are probably prime consumers as well as producers.

The Small-Scale Cheese Business, by Gianaclis Caldwell (Chelsea Green Publishing, 2010)

For those considering developing a viable farmstead or artisan cheesemaking business.

The Small-Scale Dairy, by Gianaclis Caldwell (Chelsea Green Publishing, 2014)

Focuses on milk production, especially milk intended to be used raw.

Magazines

culture — the word on cheese

If you love cheese, and I am assuming if you are reading this that you do, you must subscribe to this inspiring, gorgeous magazine. It is designed with food lovers in mind, but cheesemakers will gain from the stories of other cheesemakers from all over the world and be inspired by the beautiful photography: www.culturecheesemag.com/.

Cheese Connoisseur

Another lovely magazine devoted to the passion of eating cheese: www.cheeseconnoisseur.com.

Movies and Videos

The Cheese Nun (PBS Home Video, 2006)

I waited far too long to purchase this video (or rent it)! Not only is it a fantastic story, but you will learn some pretty cool things about cheesemaking. Even since this BBC documentary was released, Sister Noella Marcellino has continued to aid cheesemakers with her research and consultations at events such as the American Cheese Society conference, where she also serves as a cheese judge.

Artois the Goat (Bogart Reininger Films, 2008)

This is the best cheese movie I have ever seen! Okay, I know it isn't a very crowded field, but I think it will hold top honors for me for some time. It isn't just about goats or goat cheese but instead is a quirky, romantic comedy where the true ingénue is cheese. Or rather, the making of cheese.

Cheese Slices (The LifeStyle Channel, 2007–)

A DVD series out of Australia and hosted by raw-milk cheese advocate and grand personality Will Studd, *Cheese Slices* is a globe-trekking tour of cheeses, both traditional and modern, from all parts of the planet. Don't count 100 percent on its content to tell you the accurate directions for the cheeses featured, but you will still take away some great information, visuals, and inspiration.

Supplies

Get Culture, Wisconsin, USA
www.getculture.com

Supplies for home and small artisans. A part of the larger company, Dairy Connection, my favorite choice for buying supplies.

Glengarry Cheesemaking and Dairy Supply, Canada
888-816-0903
www.glengarrycheesemaking.on.ca

Small and medium-size artisans in North America. Equipment, supplies, and cultures.

New England Cheese Supply, Massachusetts, USA
413-397-2012
www.cheesemaking.com

Supplies for the home and hobby cheesemaker. Kits, supplies, cultures (in small packets), recipes on website, tech support, and blog.

The Cheesemaker, Wisconsin, USA
414-745-5483
www.thecheesemaker.com

Supplies for home and hobby cheesemakers.

ACKNOWLEDGMENTS

A GOOD BOOK DOESN'T GET WRITTEN without a lot of help from others. Thank you to my awesome readers: Vern Caldwell — husband, friend, and enabler; Eric Dolce — dedicated home cheesemaker (Temecula, California) with his eye on turning pro; Kara Olmo — uber-talented winemaker (Wooldridge Creek Winery, Applegate, Oregon) and newly minted commercial cheesemaker; Thera Lombardi — fermenter, farmer, friend, assistant, and frequent resident of Pholia Farm; Vincent Dalfonzo — musician, lover of Russian literature, farmer, friend, and food scientist. Great

thanks also to my editor Kathryn Shedrick, no matter how long I write, or how I feel that my writing skills have improved, the work of a great editor always leaves me humbled — and grateful!

A special thanks to my long-distance cheesemaker friends, Ian Treuer in Canada and Gi Claassen in San Diego, for providing some great photos of their lovingly crafted cheeses to adorn the virtual pages of this book. And, finally, thank you to New Society Publishers for believing in the need for this work and turning it into a proper book!

INDEX

as separated from curds, 9, 43, 75, 84,
  87–90, 100–101, 114–15
uses of, 45, 59, 91–93, 104, 118
See also proteins
whey, white, 119, 123, 126, 130

Y
yeasts, 10, 45, 59, 61, 68, 75, 78
yogurt, 1, 23, 44, 50, 67
  bacteria in, 57

draining of, 32–33, 59, 71, 78
recipe for, 69–71
yogurt cheeses, 23, 57, 59
  recipe for, 69–71
yogurt culture
  ABY-2C, 23
  freeze-dried, 69
  See also cultures

*G*IANACLIS HAS BEEN TEACHING all levels of cheesemaking for over a decade as well as speaking, teaching, and providing consultations about the business of small dairying and artisan cheesemaking, both on her licensed cheese dairy, Pholia Farm (www.pholiafarm.com), and across the US and abroad. She also writes regularly in *culture: the word on cheese* magazine, on her blog (www.gianacliscaldwell.com), and for other publications.

Additional books include *Mastering Artisan Cheesemaking* (Chelsea Green Publishing 2012), *The Small-Scale Dairy* (Chelsea Green 2014), and *The Small-Scale Cheese Business* (Chelsea Green 2010). She is currently writing *The Complete Dairy Goat* (Chelsea Green), which is due out in 2016.

CREDIT: BRENTON BURK.

If you have enjoyed *Mastering Basic Cheesemaking*
you might also enjoy other

BOOKS TO BUILD A NEW SOCIETY

Our books provide positive solutions for people who want to
make a difference. We specialize in:

**Food & Gardening • Resilience • Sustainable Building
Climate Change • Energy • Health & Wellness • Sustainable Living**

**Environment & Economy • Progressive Leadership • Community
Educational & Parenting Resources**

New Society Publishers
ENVIRONMENTAL BENEFITS STATEMENT

New Society Publishers has chosen to produce this book on recycled paper made
with **100% post consumer waste,** processed chlorine free, and old growth free.

For every 5,000 books printed, New Society saves the following resources:[1]

27	Trees
2,444	Pounds of Solid Waste
2,689	Gallons of Water
3,507	Kilowatt Hours of Electricity
4,442	Pounds of Greenhouse Gases
19	Pounds of HAPs, VOCs, and AOX Combined
7	Cubic Yards of Landfill Space

[1]Environmental benefits are calculated based on research done by the Environmental Defense Fund
and other members of the Paper Task Force who study the environmental impacts of the paper
industry.

For a full list of NSP's titles, please call 1-800-567-6772 *or check out our website at:*
www.newsociety.com